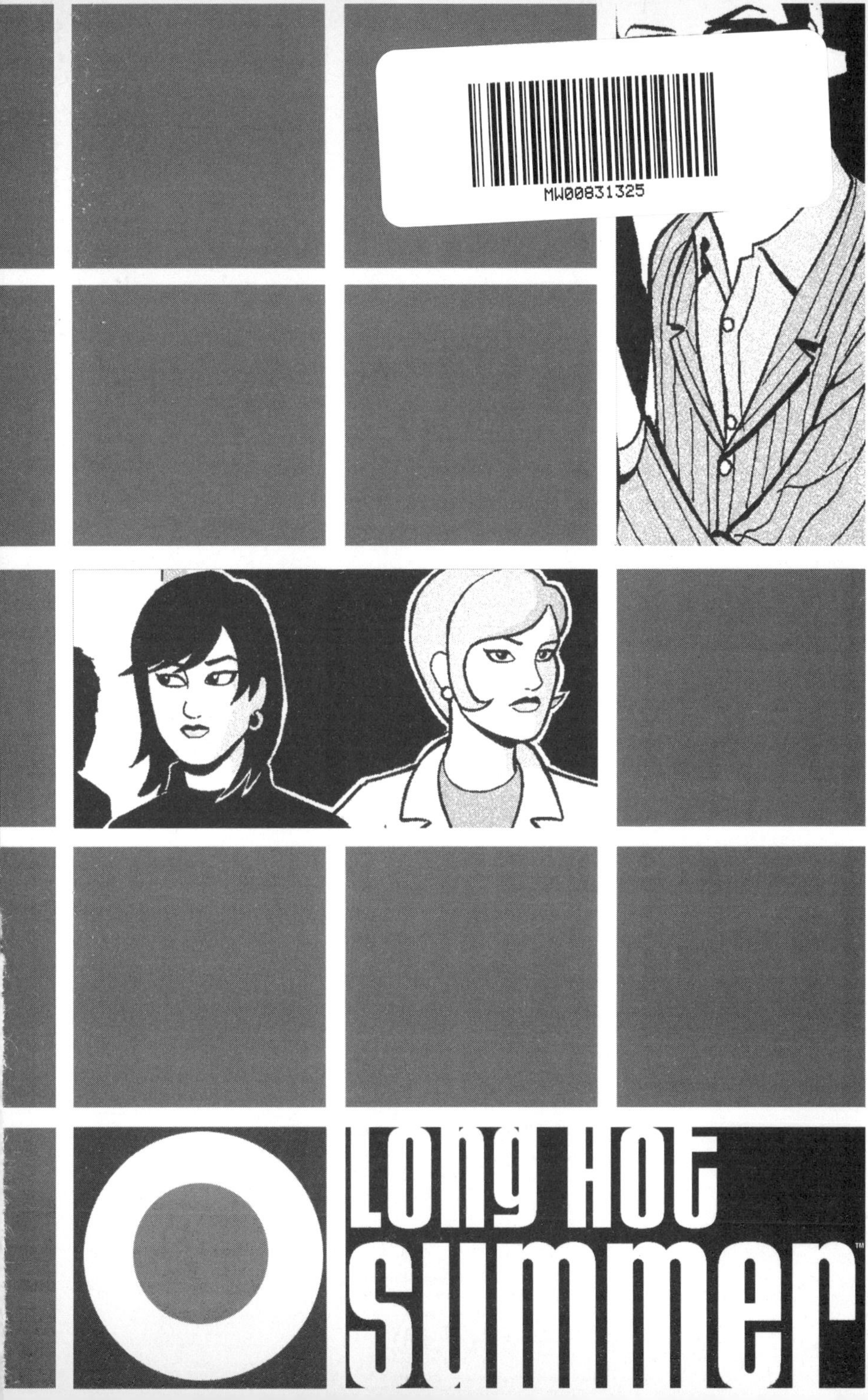

Long Hot Summer™

IMAGE COMICS, INC.

Erik Larsen - Publisher
Todd McFarlane - President
Marc Silvestri - CEO
Jim Valentino - Vice-President

Eric Stephenson - Executive Director
Missie Miranda - Controller
Brett Evans - Production Manager
Jim Demonakos - Pr & Marketing Coordinator
Allen Hui - Production Artist
Joe Keatinge - Traffic Manager
Mia MacHatton - Administrative Assistant
Jonathan Chan - Production Assistant

Image Comics, Inc.
1942 University Ave
Suite 305
Berkeley, CA 94704

www.imagecomics.com

First Printing, 2005.

Printed in Canada.

LONG HOT SUMMER™

written by
ERIC
STEPHENSON

illustrated & lettered by
JAMIE
MCKELVIE

designed by
LAURENN
MCCUBBIN

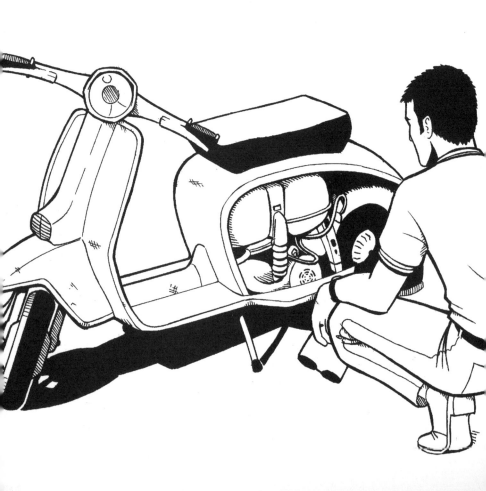

FIGARO
FIGARO

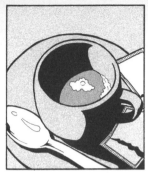

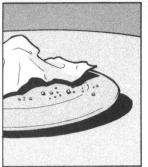

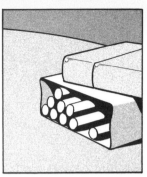

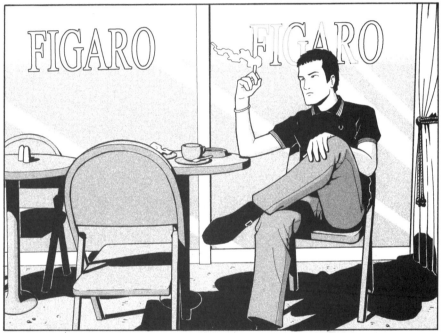

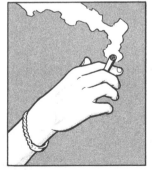

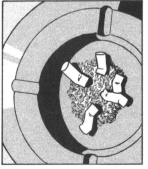

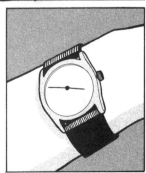

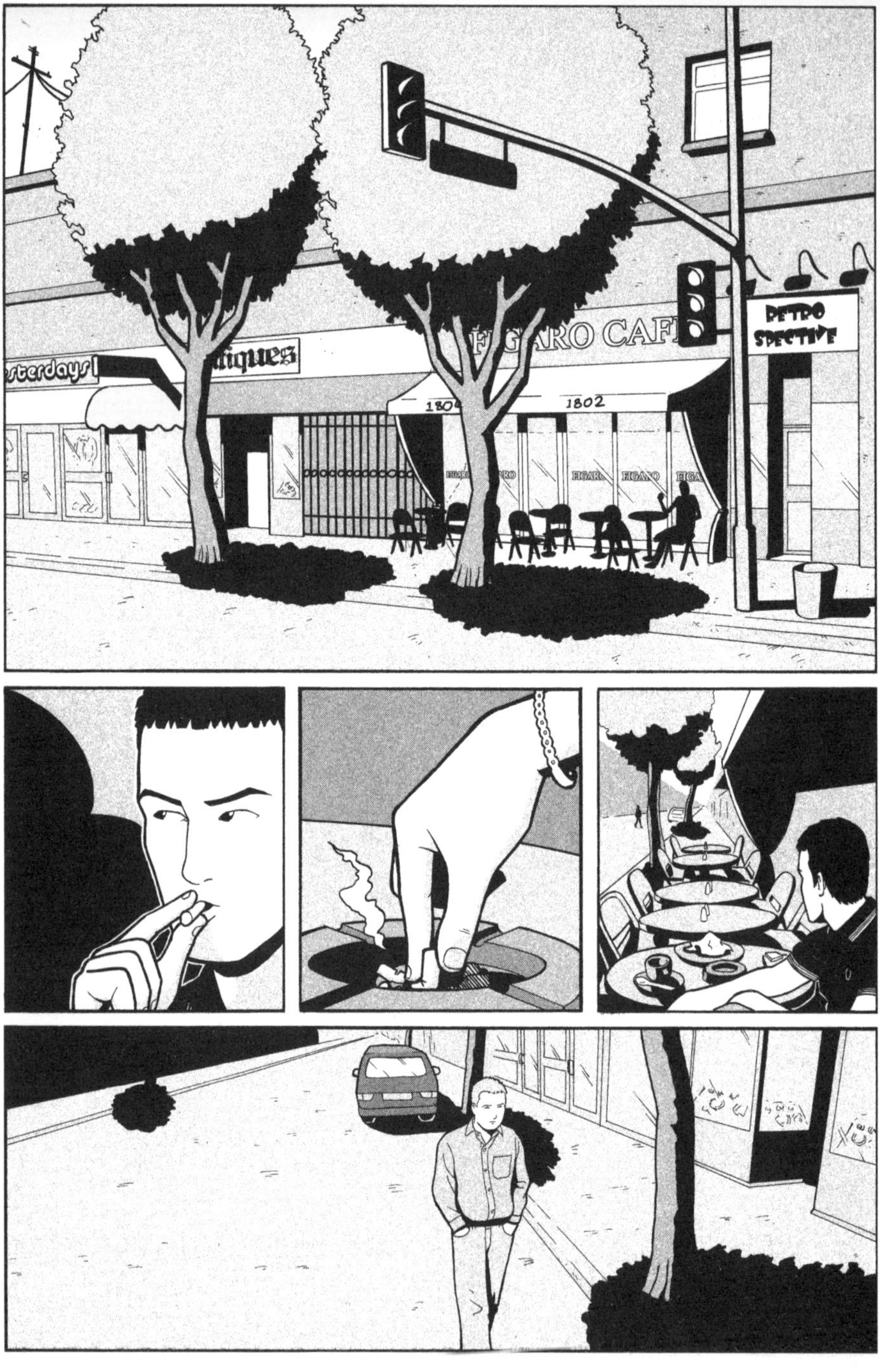
FIGARO CAFE
RETRO SPECTIVE
1804
1802
FIGARO

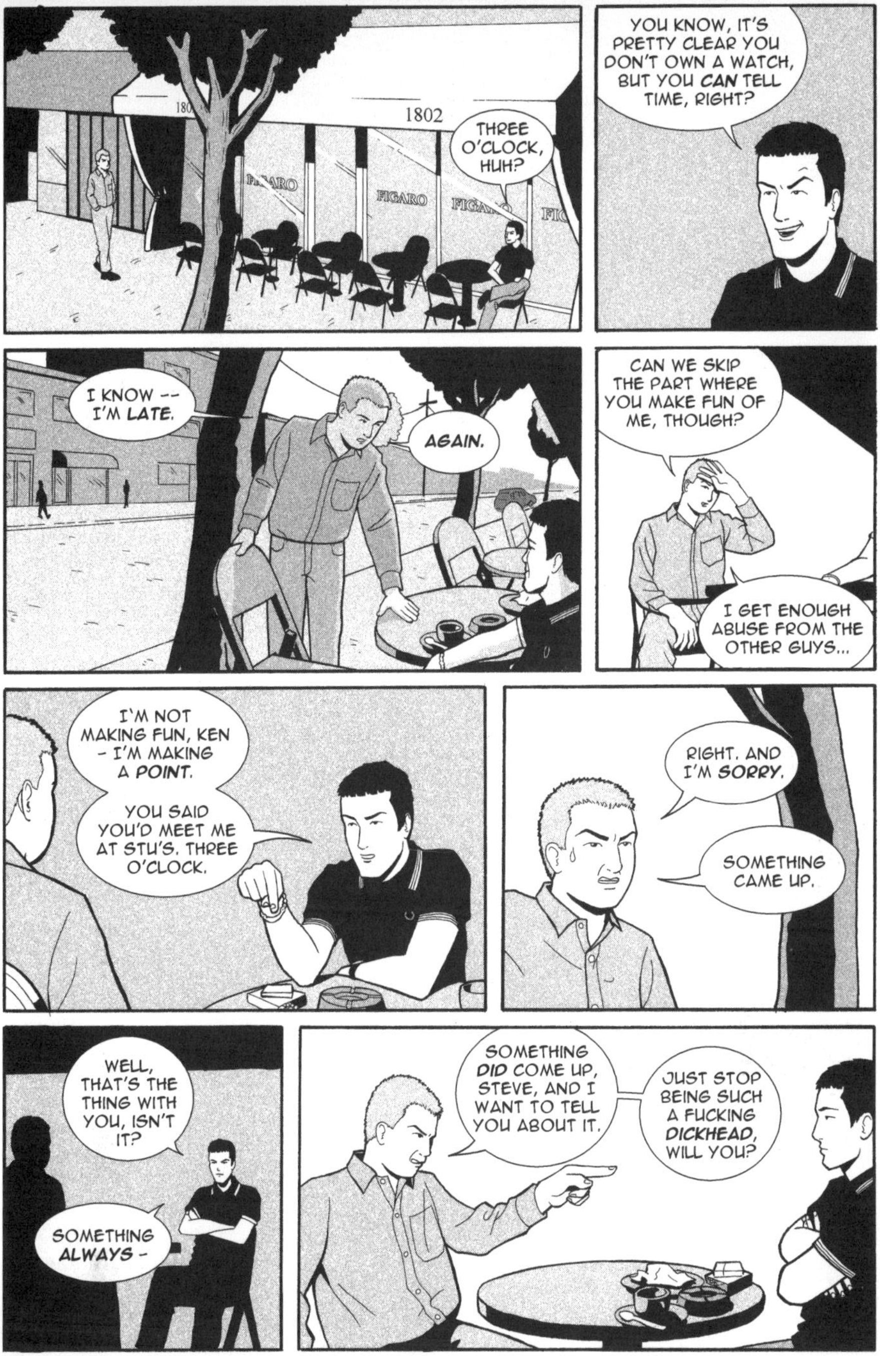
1802
FIGARO
THREE O'CLOCK, HUH?
YOU KNOW, IT'S PRETTY CLEAR YOU DON'T OWN A WATCH, BUT YOU CAN TELL TIME, RIGHT?
I KNOW -- I'M LATE.
AGAIN.
CAN WE SKIP THE PART WHERE YOU MAKE FUN OF ME, THOUGH?
I GET ENOUGH ABUSE FROM THE OTHER GUYS...
I'M NOT MAKING FUN, KEN - I'M MAKING A POINT.
YOU SAID YOU'D MEET ME AT STU'S. THREE O'CLOCK.
RIGHT. AND I'M SORRY.
SOMETHING CAME UP.
WELL, THAT'S THE THING WITH YOU, ISN'T IT?
SOMETHING ALWAYS -
SOMETHING DID COME UP, STEVE, AND I WANT TO TELL YOU ABOUT IT.
JUST STOP BEING SUCH A FUCKING DICKHEAD, WILL YOU?

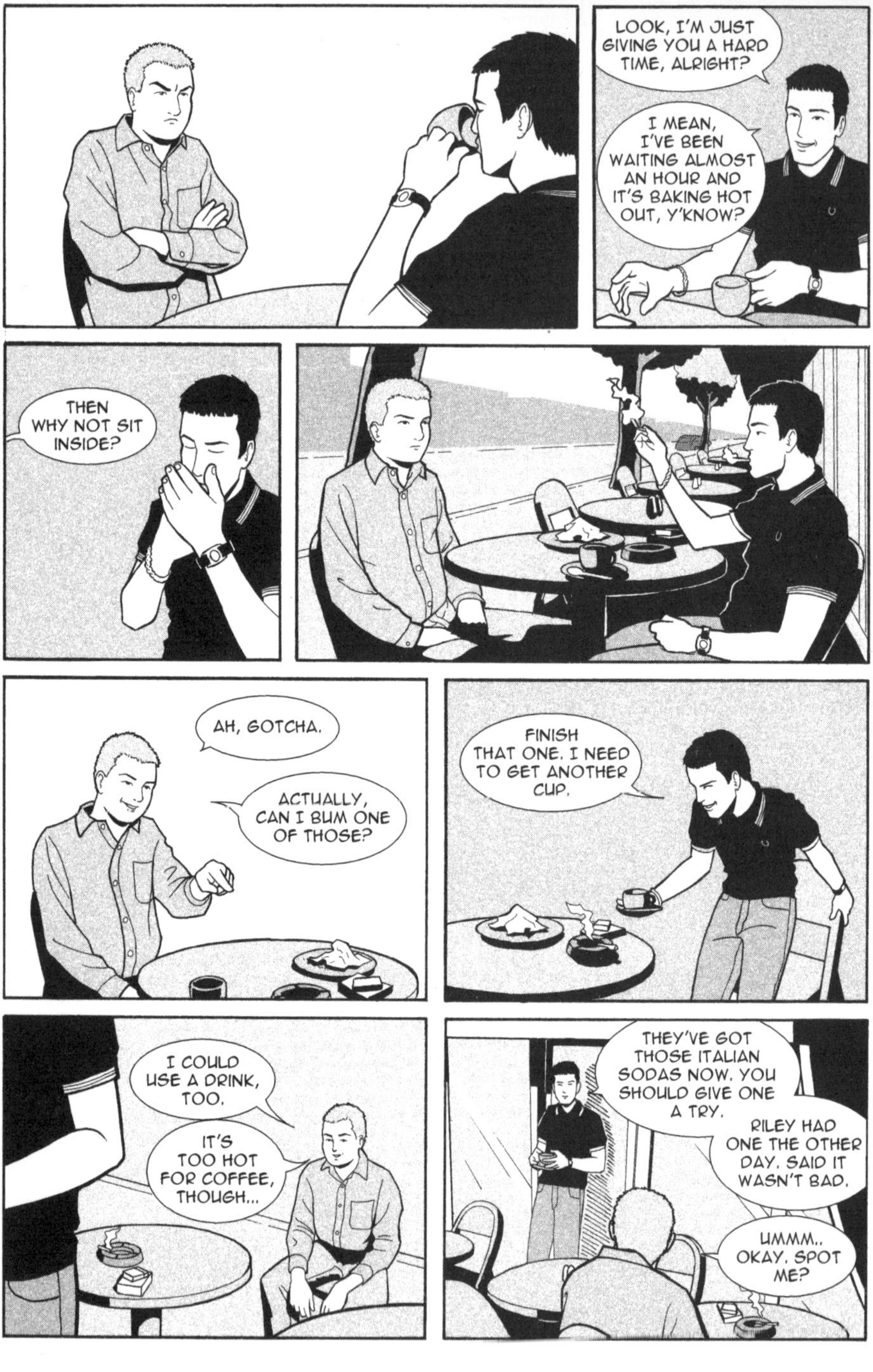
LOOK, I'M JUST GIVING YOU A HARD TIME, ALRIGHT?
I MEAN, I'VE BEEN WAITING ALMOST AN HOUR AND IT'S BAKING HOT OUT, Y'KNOW?
THEN WHY NOT SIT INSIDE?
AH, GOTCHA.
ACTUALLY, CAN I BUM ONE OF THOSE?
FINISH THAT ONE. I NEED TO GET ANOTHER CUP.
I COULD USE A DRINK, TOO.
IT'S TOO HOT FOR COFFEE, THOUGH...
THEY'VE GOT THOSE ITALIAN SODAS NOW. YOU SHOULD GIVE ONE A TRY.
RILEY HAD ONE THE OTHER DAY. SAID IT WASN'T BAD.
UMMM.. OKAY. SPOT ME?

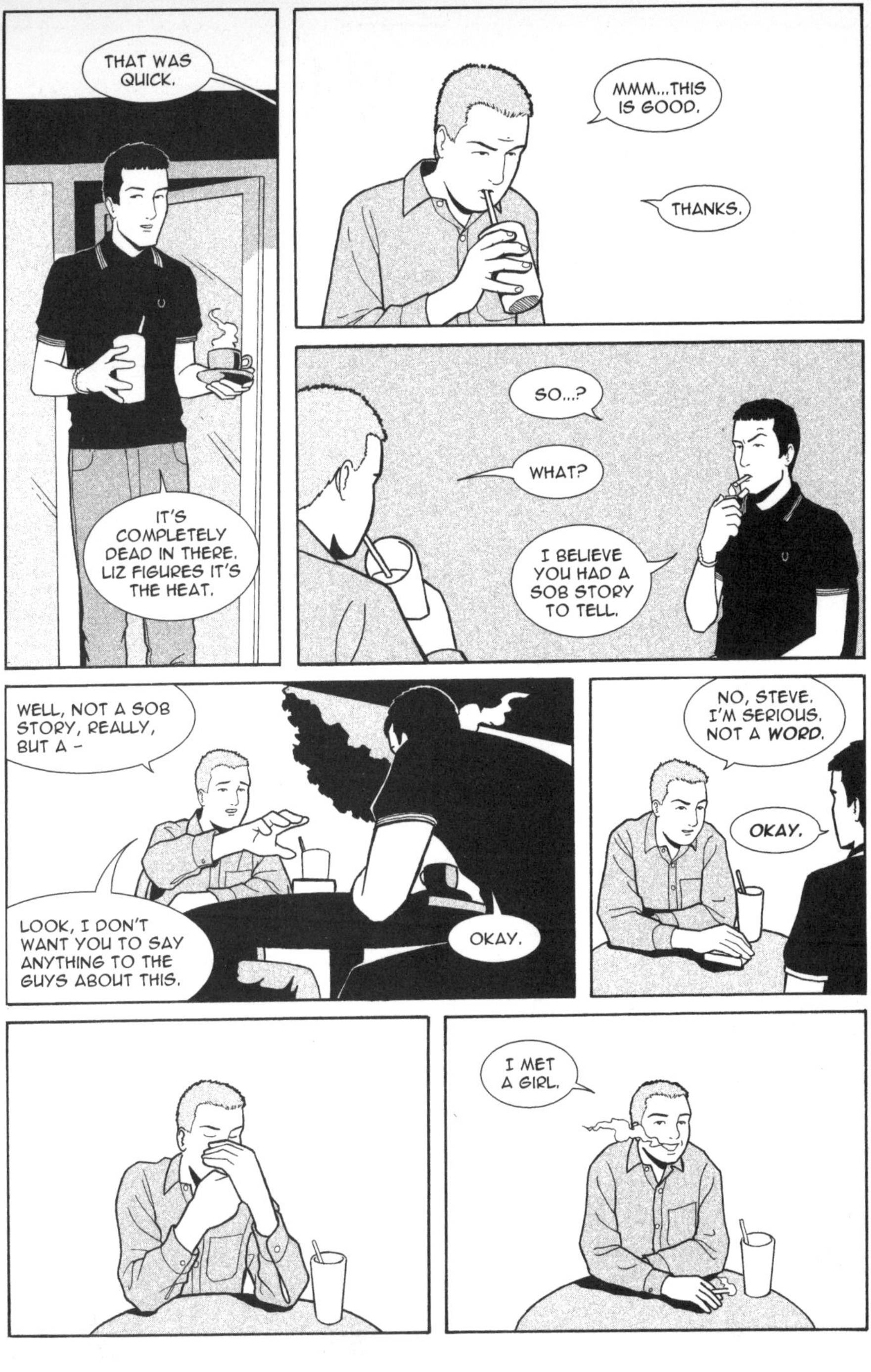
THAT WAS QUICK.
IT'S COMPLETELY DEAD IN THERE. LIZ FIGURES IT'S THE HEAT.
MMM...THIS IS GOOD.
THANKS.
SO...?
WHAT?
I BELIEVE YOU HAD A SOB STORY TO TELL.
WELL, NOT A SOB STORY, REALLY, BUT A -
LOOK, I DON'T WANT YOU TO SAY ANYTHING TO THE GUYS ABOUT THIS.
OKAY.
NO, STEVE. I'M SERIOUS. NOT A **WORD**.
OKAY.
I MET A GIRL.

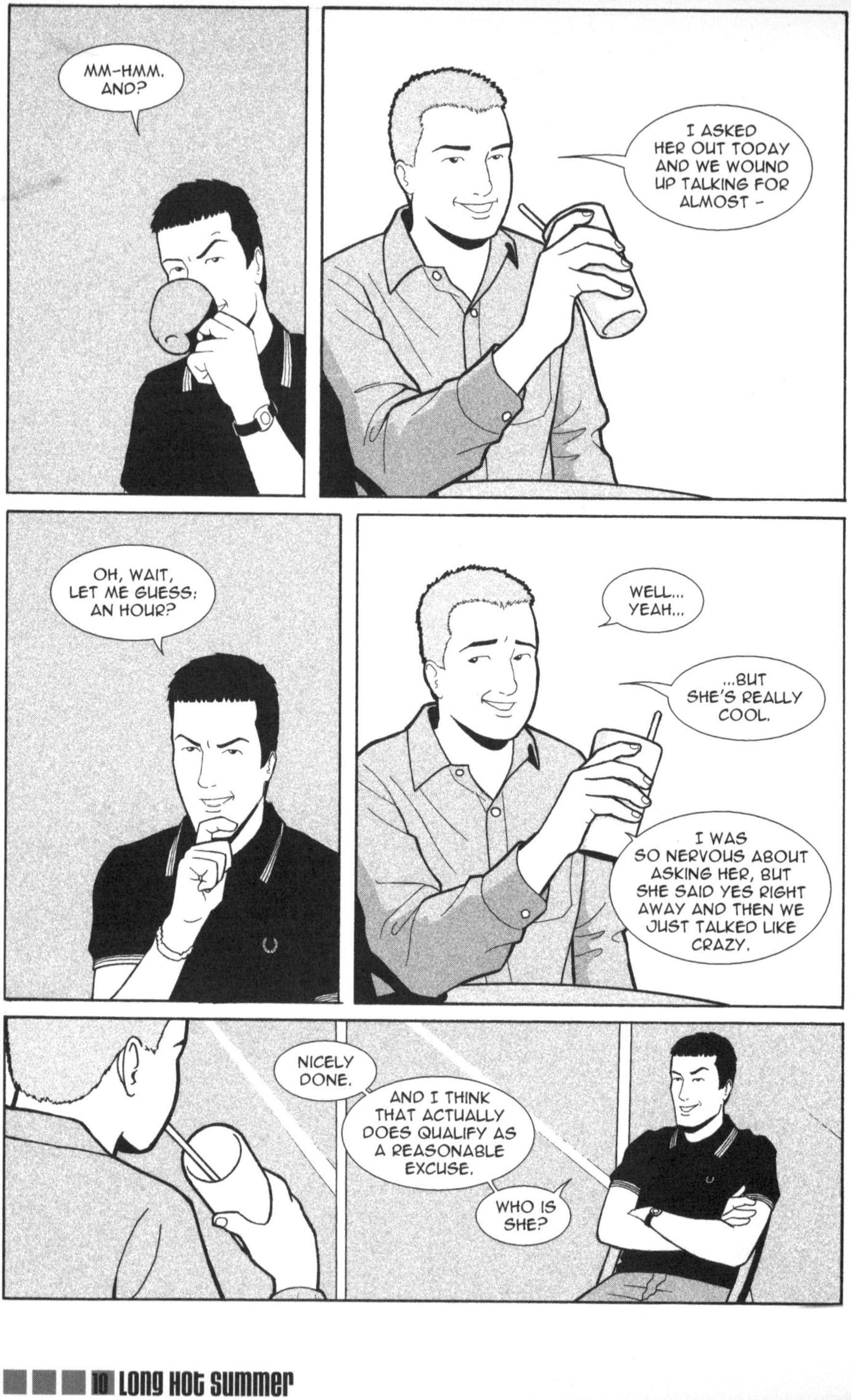
MM-HMM. AND?
I ASKED HER OUT TODAY AND WE WOUND UP TALKING FOR ALMOST -
OH, WAIT, LET ME GUESS: AN HOUR?
WELL... YEAH...
...BUT SHE'S REALLY COOL.
I WAS SO NERVOUS ABOUT ASKING HER, BUT SHE SAID YES RIGHT AWAY AND THEN WE JUST TALKED LIKE CRAZY.
NICELY DONE.
AND I THINK THAT ACTUALLY DOES QUALIFY AS A REASONABLE EXCUSE.
WHO IS SHE?

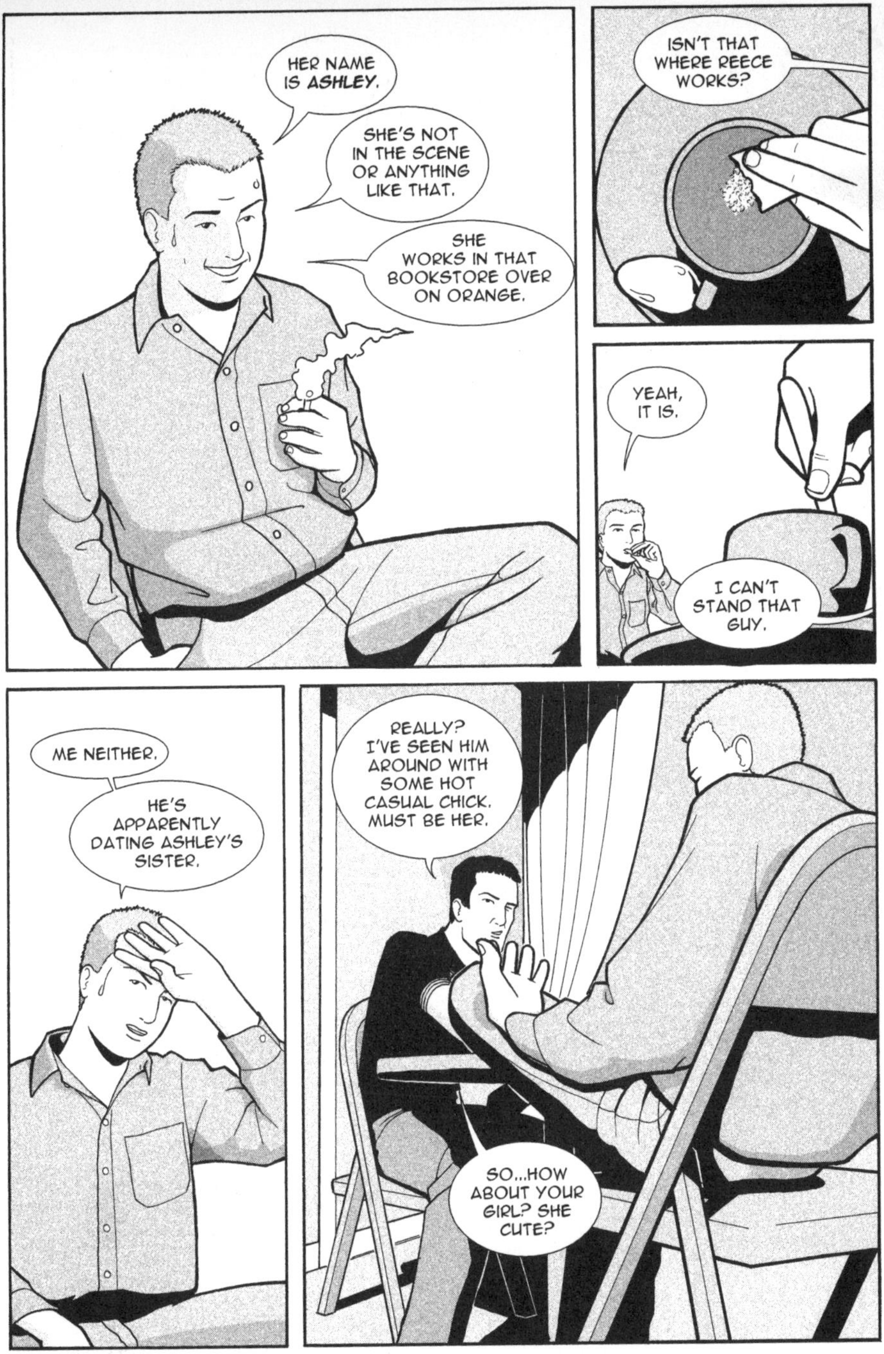
HER NAME IS ASHLEY.
SHE'S NOT IN THE SCENE OR ANYTHING LIKE THAT.
SHE WORKS IN THAT BOOKSTORE OVER ON ORANGE.
ISN'T THAT WHERE REECE WORKS?
YEAH, IT IS.
I CAN'T STAND THAT GUY.
ME NEITHER.
HE'S APPARENTLY DATING ASHLEY'S SISTER.
REALLY? I'VE SEEN HIM AROUND WITH SOME HOT CASUAL CHICK. MUST BE HER.
SO...HOW ABOUT YOUR GIRL? SHE CUTE?

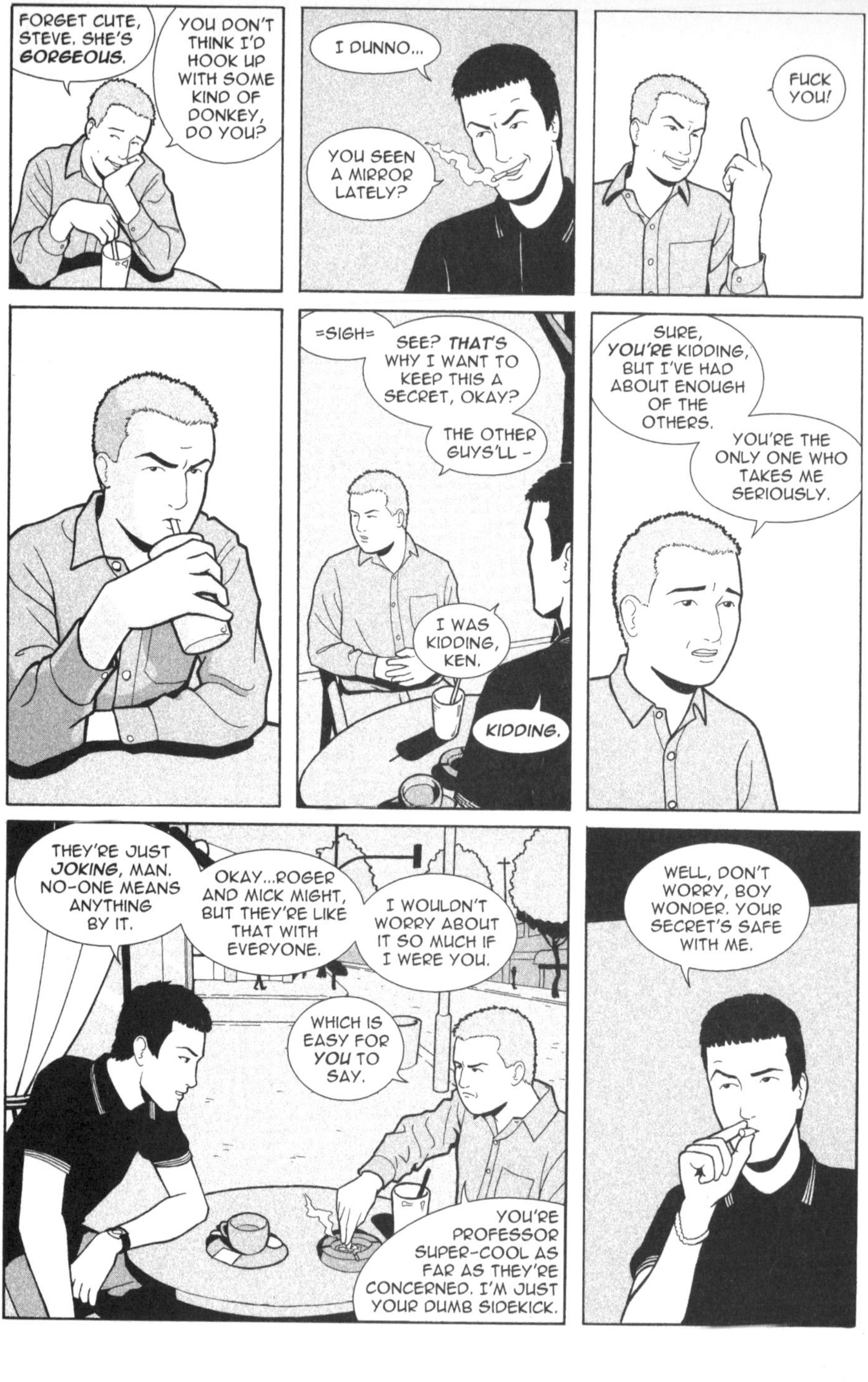
FORGET CUTE, STEVE. SHE'S GORGEOUS.
YOU DON'T THINK I'D HOOK UP WITH SOME KIND OF DONKEY, DO YOU?
I DUNNO...
YOU SEEN A MIRROR LATELY?
FUCK YOU!
=SIGH=
SEE? THAT'S WHY I WANT TO KEEP THIS A SECRET, OKAY?
THE OTHER GUYS'LL -
I WAS KIDDING, KEN.
KIDDING.
SURE, YOU'RE KIDDING, BUT I'VE HAD ABOUT ENOUGH OF THE OTHERS.
YOU'RE THE ONLY ONE WHO TAKES ME SERIOUSLY.
THEY'RE JUST JOKING, MAN. NO-ONE MEANS ANYTHING BY IT.
OKAY...ROGER AND MICK MIGHT, BUT THEY'RE LIKE THAT WITH EVERYONE.
I WOULDN'T WORRY ABOUT IT SO MUCH IF I WERE YOU.
WHICH IS EASY FOR YOU TO SAY.
YOU'RE PROFESSOR SUPER-COOL AS FAR AS THEY'RE CONCERNED. I'M JUST YOUR DUMB SIDEKICK.
WELL, DON'T WORRY, BOY WONDER. YOUR SECRET'S SAFE WITH ME.

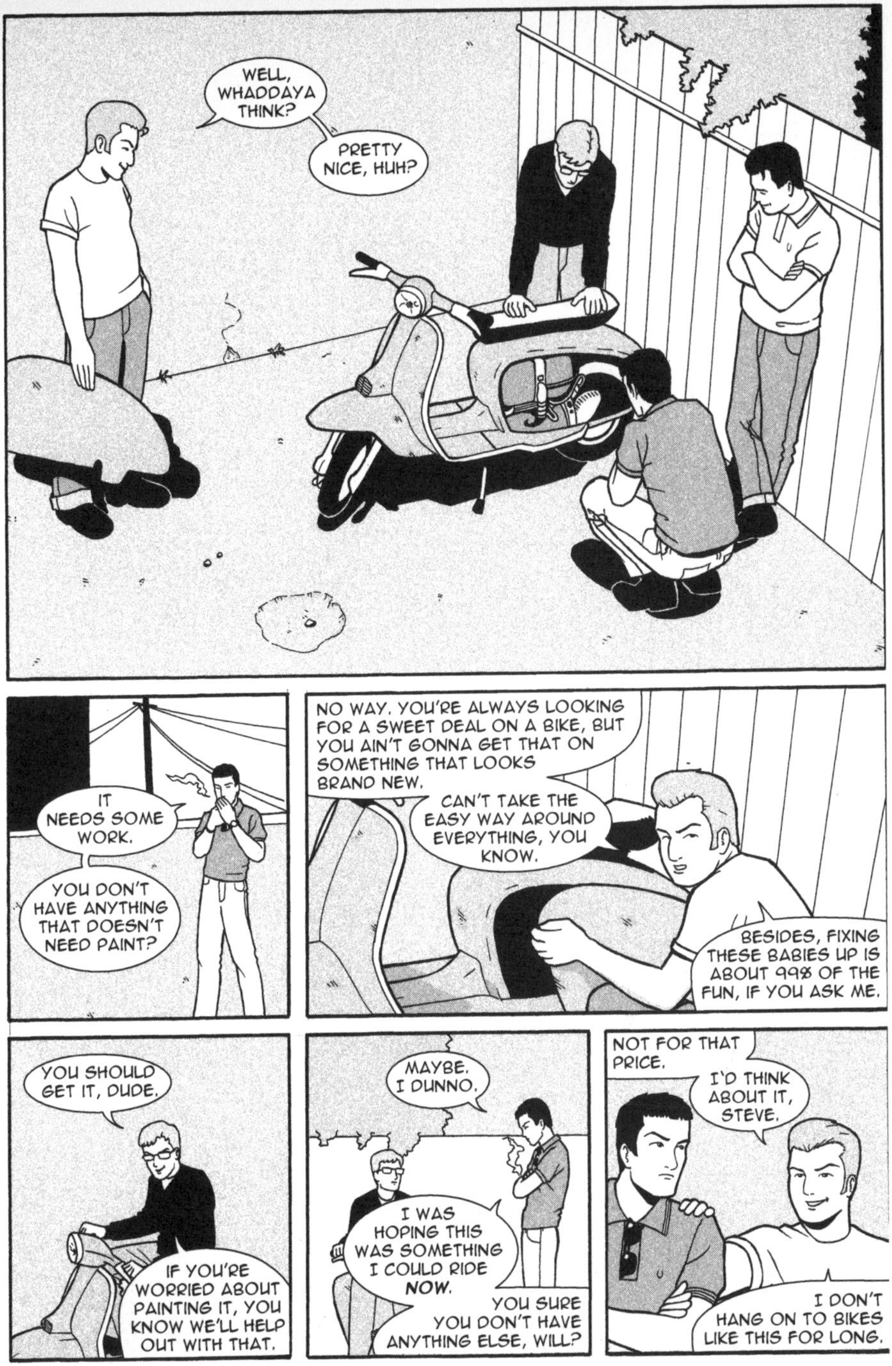

WELL, WHADDAYA THINK?
PRETTY NICE, HUH?
IT NEEDS SOME WORK.
YOU DON'T HAVE ANYTHING THAT DOESN'T NEED PAINT?
NO WAY. YOU'RE ALWAYS LOOKING FOR A SWEET DEAL ON A BIKE, BUT YOU AIN'T GONNA GET THAT ON SOMETHING THAT LOOKS BRAND NEW.
CAN'T TAKE THE EASY WAY AROUND EVERYTHING, YOU KNOW.
BESIDES, FIXING THESE BABIES UP IS ABOUT 99% OF THE FUN, IF YOU ASK ME.
YOU SHOULD GET IT, DUDE.
IF YOU'RE WORRIED ABOUT PAINTING IT, YOU KNOW WE'LL HELP OUT WITH THAT.
MAYBE. I DUNNO.
I WAS HOPING THIS WAS SOMETHING I COULD RIDE **NOW**.
YOU SURE YOU DON'T HAVE ANYTHING ELSE, WILL?
NOT FOR THAT PRICE.
I'D THINK ABOUT IT, STEVE.
I DON'T HANG ON TO BIKES LIKE THIS FOR LONG.

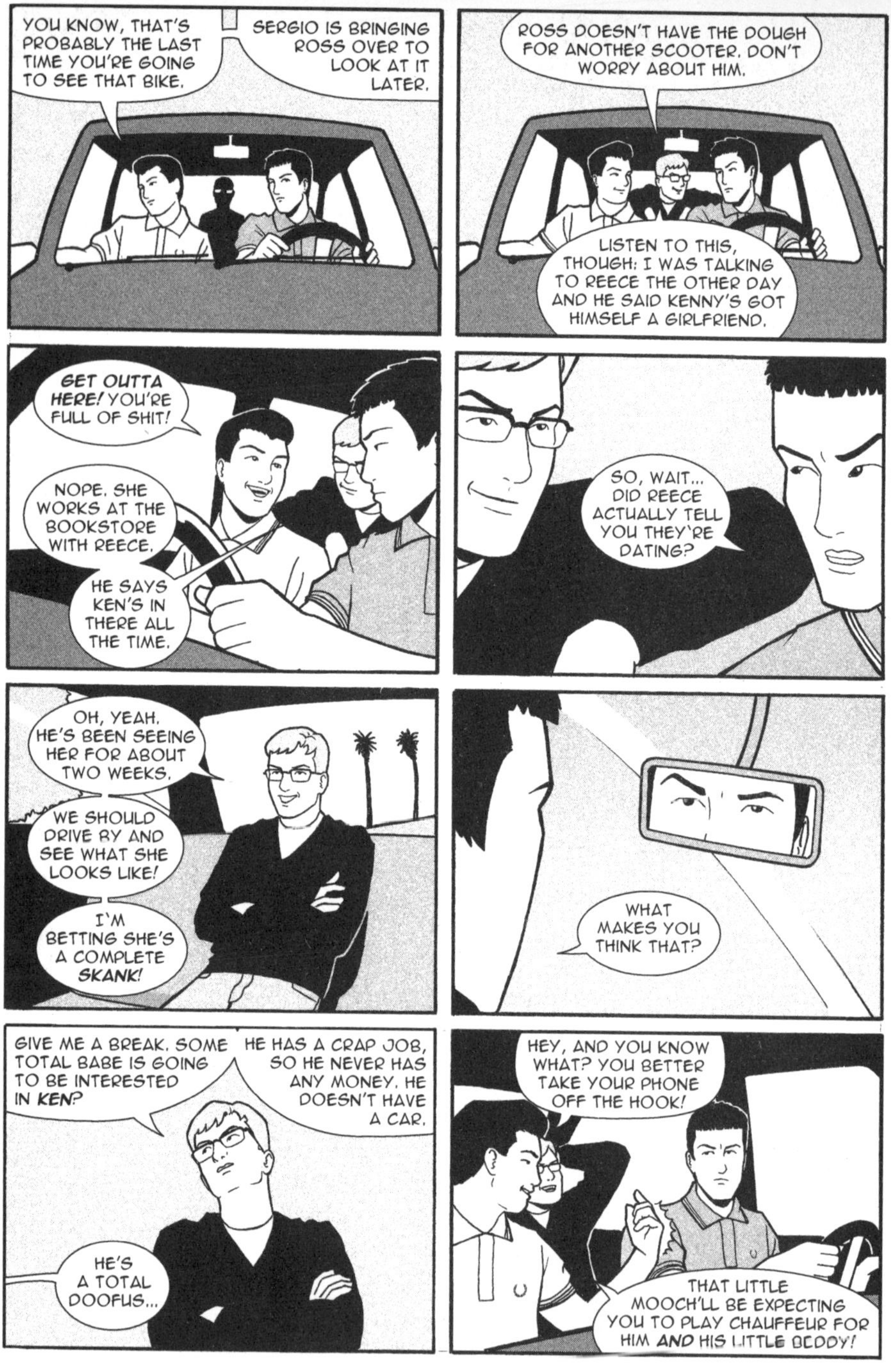
YOU KNOW, THAT'S PROBABLY THE LAST TIME YOU'RE GOING TO SEE THAT BIKE.
SERGIO IS BRINGING ROSS OVER TO LOOK AT IT LATER.
ROSS DOESN'T HAVE THE DOUGH FOR ANOTHER SCOOTER. DON'T WORRY ABOUT HIM.
LISTEN TO THIS, THOUGH: I WAS TALKING TO REECE THE OTHER DAY AND HE SAID KENNY'S GOT HIMSELF A GIRLFRIEND.
GET OUTTA HERE! YOU'RE FULL OF SHIT!
NOPE. SHE WORKS AT THE BOOKSTORE WITH REECE.
HE SAYS KEN'S IN THERE ALL THE TIME.
SO, WAIT... DID REECE ACTUALLY TELL YOU THEY'RE DATING?
OH, YEAH. HE'S BEEN SEEING HER FOR ABOUT TWO WEEKS.
WE SHOULD DRIVE BY AND SEE WHAT SHE LOOKS LIKE!
I'M BETTING SHE'S A COMPLETE SKANK!
WHAT MAKES YOU THINK THAT?
GIVE ME A BREAK. SOME TOTAL BABE IS GOING TO BE INTERESTED IN KEN?
HE HAS A CRAP JOB, SO HE NEVER HAS ANY MONEY. HE DOESN'T HAVE A CAR.
HE'S A TOTAL DOOFUS...
HEY, AND YOU KNOW WHAT? YOU BETTER TAKE YOUR PHONE OFF THE HOOK!
THAT LITTLE MOOCH'LL BE EXPECTING YOU TO PLAY CHAUFFEUR FOR HIM AND HIS LITTLE BEDDY!

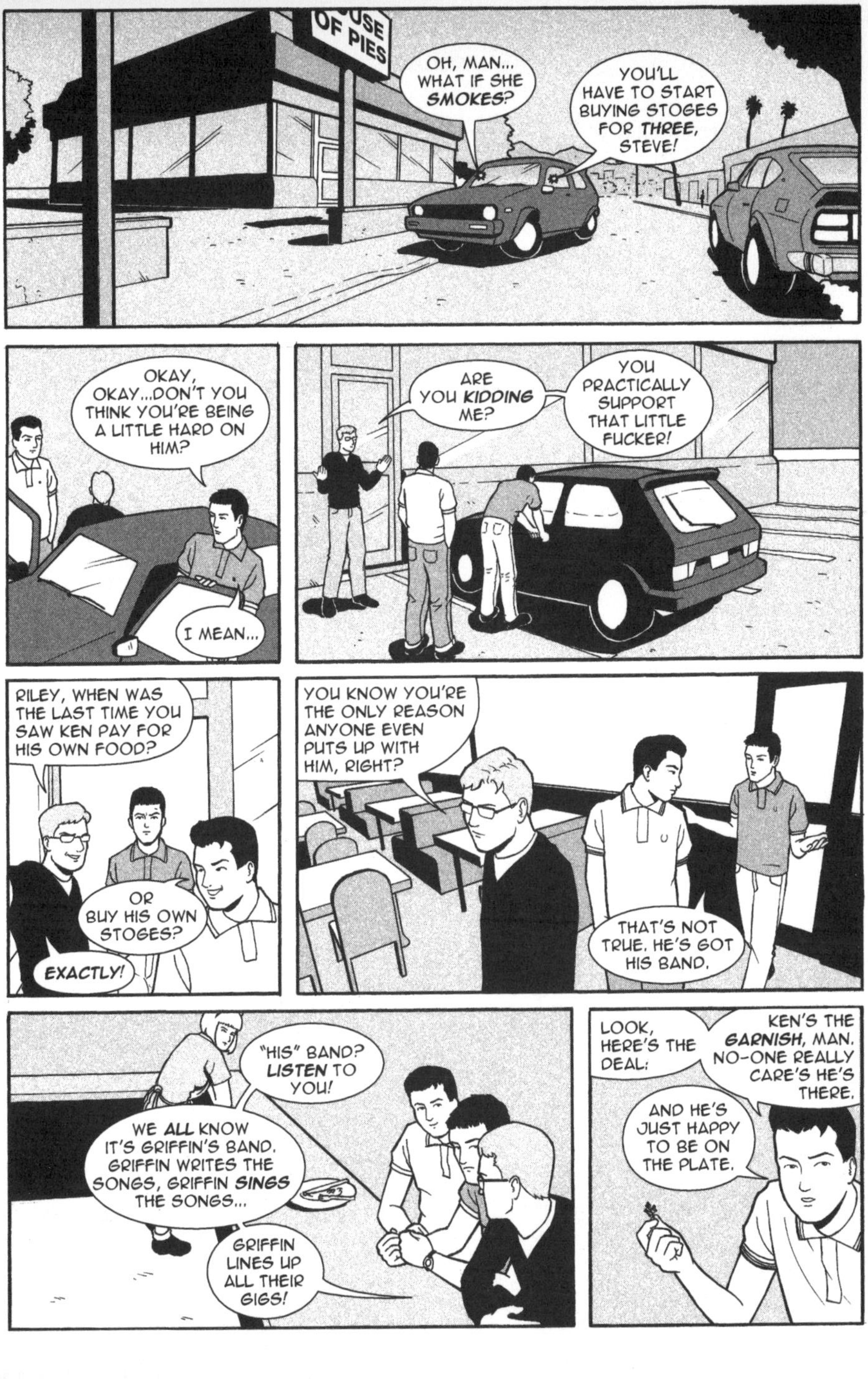
OUSE OF PIES
OH, MAN... WHAT IF SHE SMOKES?
YOU'LL HAVE TO START BUYING STOGES FOR THREE, STEVE!
OKAY, OKAY...DON'T YOU THINK YOU'RE BEING A LITTLE HARD ON HIM?
I MEAN...
ARE YOU KIDDING ME?
YOU PRACTICALLY SUPPORT THAT LITTLE FUCKER!
RILEY, WHEN WAS THE LAST TIME YOU SAW KEN PAY FOR HIS OWN FOOD?
OR BUY HIS OWN STOGES?
EXACTLY!
YOU KNOW YOU'RE THE ONLY REASON ANYONE EVEN PUTS UP WITH HIM, RIGHT?
THAT'S NOT TRUE. HE'S GOT HIS BAND.
"HIS" BAND? LISTEN TO YOU!
WE ALL KNOW IT'S GRIFFIN'S BAND. GRIFFIN WRITES THE SONGS, GRIFFIN SINGS THE SONGS...
GRIFFIN LINES UP ALL THEIR GIGS!
LOOK, HERE'S THE DEAL:
KEN'S THE GARNISH, MAN. NO-ONE REALLY CARE'S HE'S THERE.
AND HE'S JUST HAPPY TO BE ON THE PLATE.

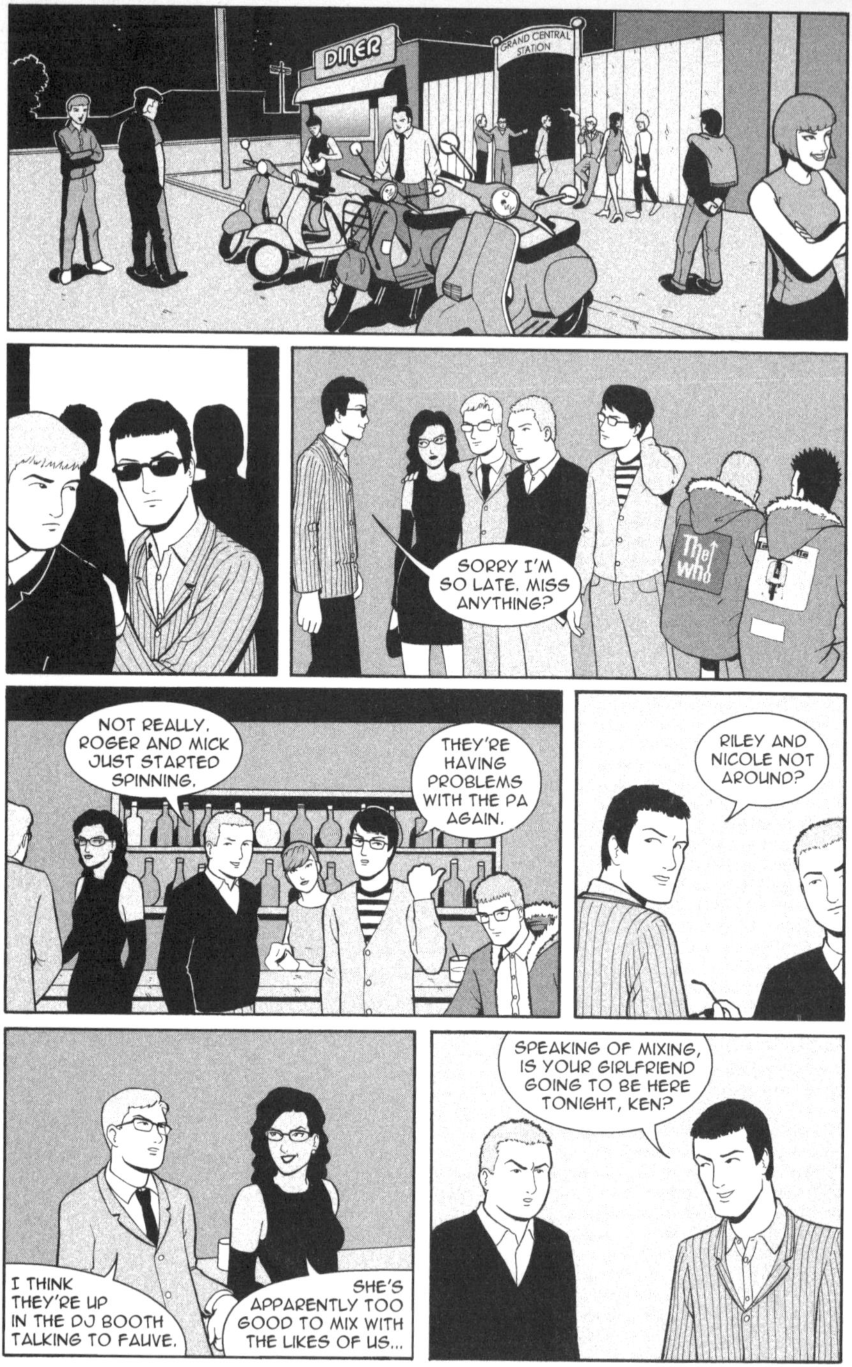
DINER
GRAND CENTRAL STATION
The Who
SORRY I'M SO LATE. MISS ANYTHING?
NOT REALLY. ROGER AND MICK JUST STARTED SPINNING.
THEY'RE HAVING PROBLEMS WITH THE PA AGAIN.
RILEY AND NICOLE NOT AROUND?
I THINK THEY'RE UP IN THE DJ BOOTH TALKING TO FAUVE.
SHE'S APPARENTLY TOO GOOD TO MIX WITH THE LIKES OF US...
SPEAKING OF MIXING, IS YOUR GIRLFRIEND GOING TO BE HERE TONIGHT, KEN?

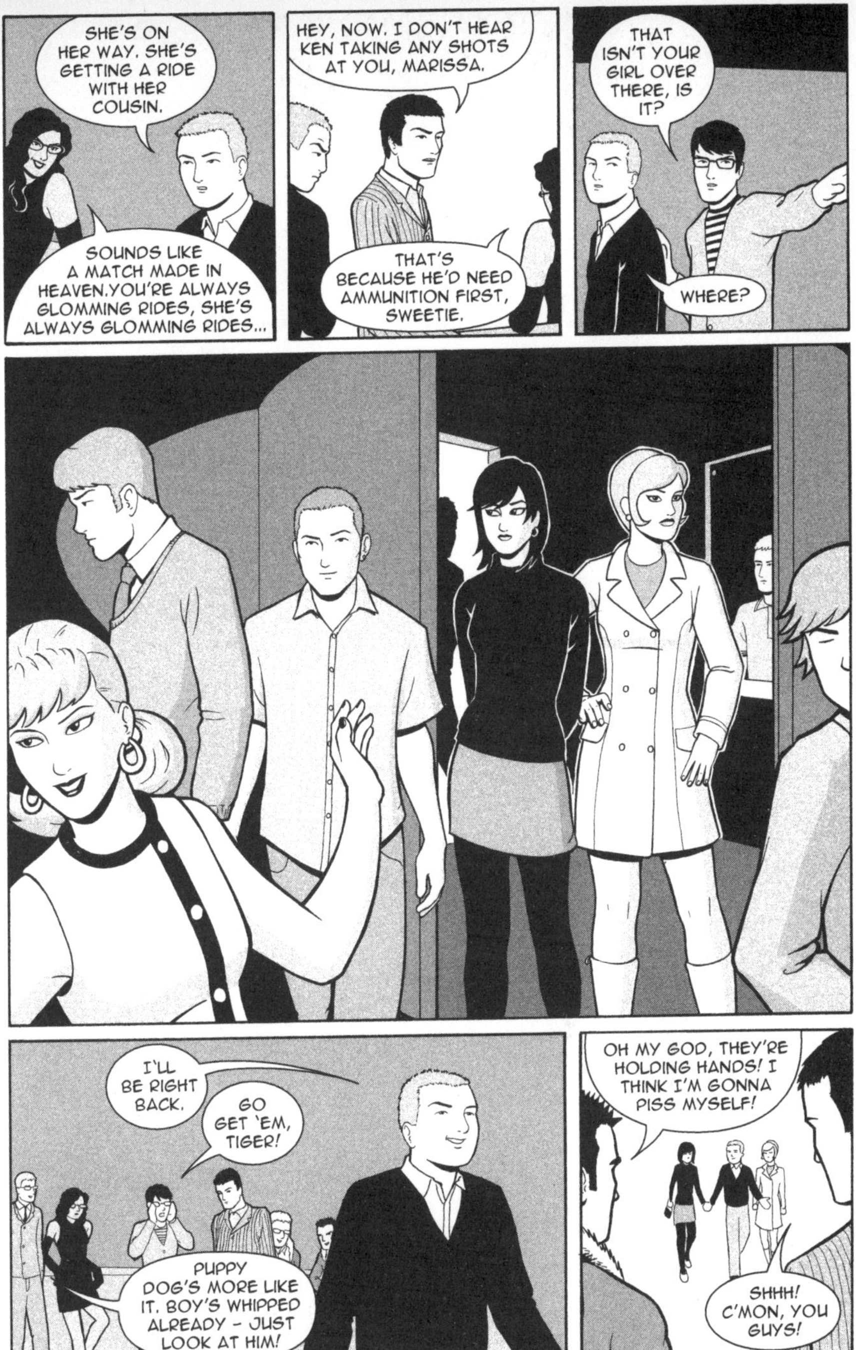
SHE'S ON HER WAY. SHE'S GETTING A RIDE WITH HER COUSIN.
SOUNDS LIKE A MATCH MADE IN HEAVEN. YOU'RE ALWAYS GLOMMING RIDES, SHE'S ALWAYS GLOMMING RIDES...
HEY, NOW. I DON'T HEAR KEN TAKING ANY SHOTS AT YOU, MARISSA.
THAT'S BECAUSE HE'D NEED AMMUNITION FIRST, SWEETIE.
THAT ISN'T YOUR GIRL OVER THERE, IS IT?
WHERE?
I'LL BE RIGHT BACK.
GO GET 'EM, TIGER!
PUPPY DOG'S MORE LIKE IT. BOY'S WHIPPED ALREADY - JUST LOOK AT HIM!
OH MY GOD, THEY'RE HOLDING HANDS! I THINK I'M GONNA PISS MYSELF!
SHHH! C'MON, YOU GUYS!

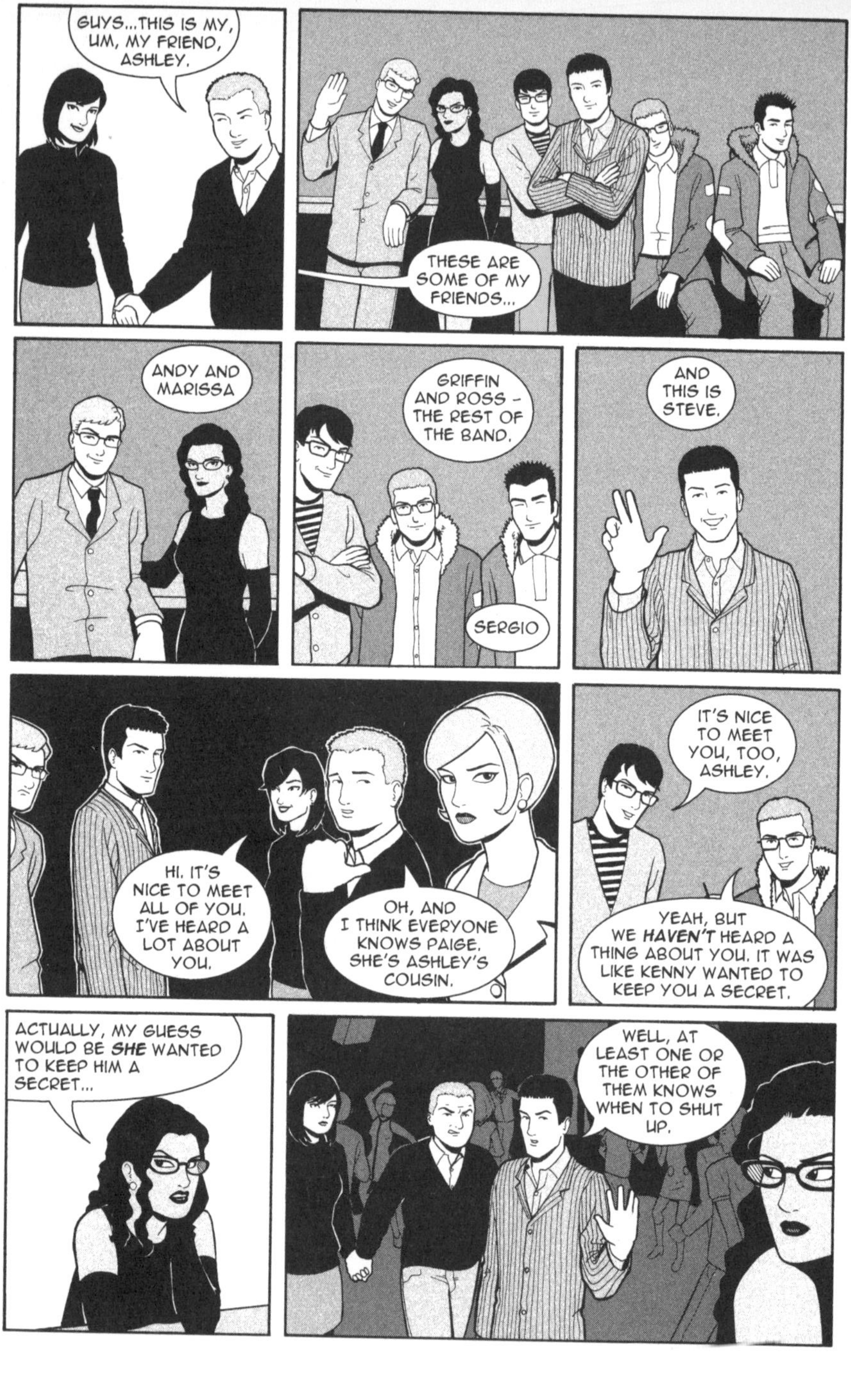
GUYS...THIS IS MY, UM, MY FRIEND, ASHLEY.
THESE ARE SOME OF MY FRIENDS...
ANDY AND MARISSA
GRIFFIN AND ROSS – THE REST OF THE BAND.
SERGIO
AND THIS IS STEVE.
HI. IT'S NICE TO MEET ALL OF YOU. I'VE HEARD A LOT ABOUT YOU.
OH, AND I THINK EVERYONE KNOWS PAIGE. SHE'S ASHLEY'S COUSIN.
IT'S NICE TO MEET YOU, TOO, ASHLEY.
YEAH, BUT WE **HAVEN'T** HEARD A THING ABOUT YOU. IT WAS LIKE KENNY WANTED TO KEEP YOU A SECRET.
ACTUALLY, MY GUESS WOULD BE **SHE** WANTED TO KEEP HIM A SECRET...
WELL, AT LEAST ONE OR THE OTHER OF THEM KNOWS WHEN TO SHUT UP.

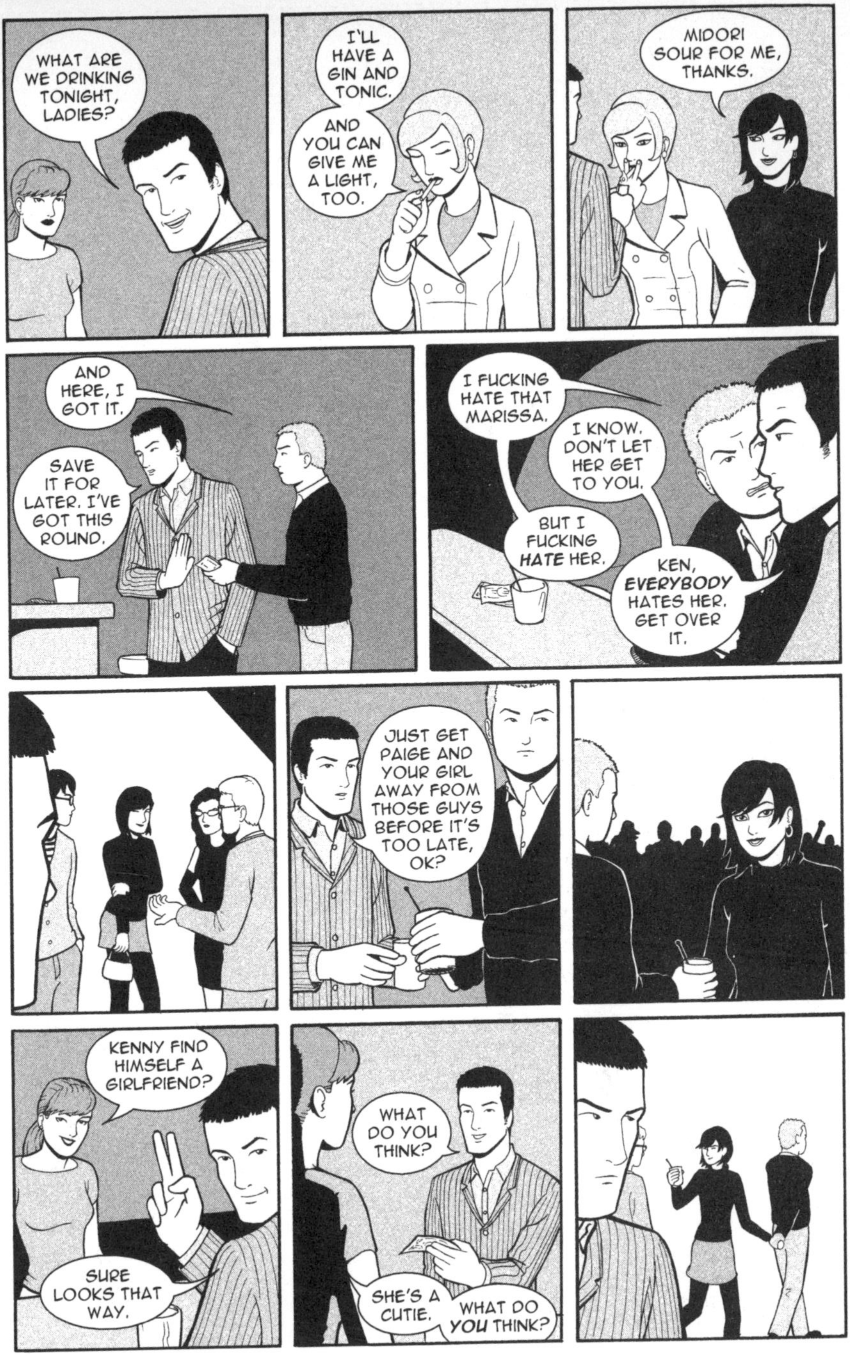
WHAT ARE WE DRINKING TONIGHT, LADIES?
I'LL HAVE A GIN AND TONIC.
AND YOU CAN GIVE ME A LIGHT, TOO.
MIDORI SOUR FOR ME, THANKS.
AND HERE, I GOT IT.
SAVE IT FOR LATER. I'VE GOT THIS ROUND.
I FUCKING HATE THAT MARISSA.
I KNOW. DON'T LET HER GET TO YOU.
BUT I FUCKING HATE HER.
KEN, EVERYBODY HATES HER. GET OVER IT.
JUST GET PAIGE AND YOUR GIRL AWAY FROM THOSE GUYS BEFORE IT'S TOO LATE, OK?
KENNY FIND HIMSELF A GIRLFRIEND?
SURE LOOKS THAT WAY.
WHAT DO YOU THINK?
SHE'S A CUTIE.
WHAT DO YOU THINK?

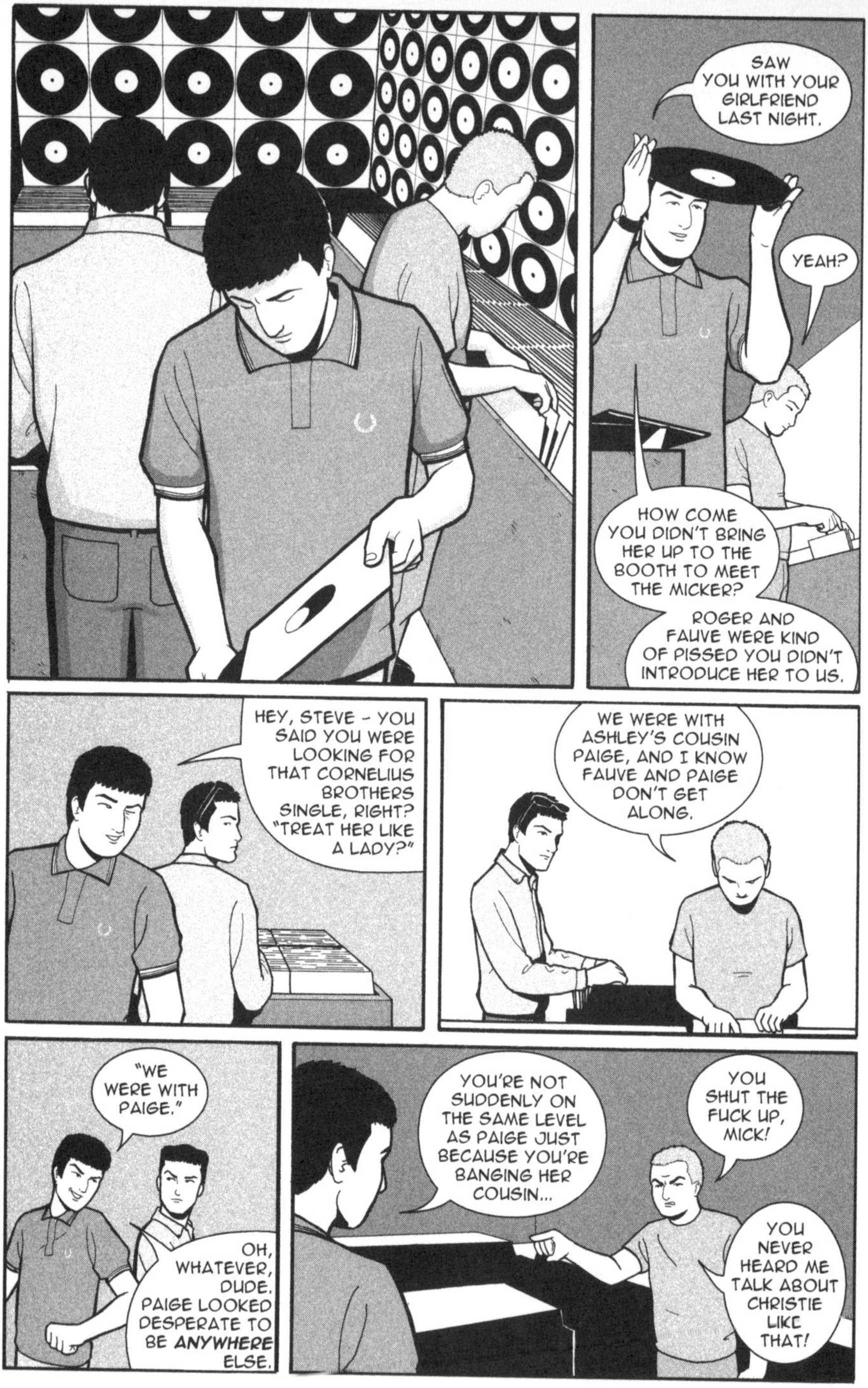
SAW YOU WITH YOUR GIRLFRIEND LAST NIGHT.
YEAH?
HOW COME YOU DIDN'T BRING HER UP TO THE BOOTH TO MEET THE MICKER?
ROGER AND FAUVE WERE KIND OF PISSED YOU DIDN'T INTRODUCE HER TO US.
HEY, STEVE - YOU SAID YOU WERE LOOKING FOR THAT CORNELIUS BROTHERS SINGLE, RIGHT? "TREAT HER LIKE A LADY?"
WE WERE WITH ASHLEY'S COUSIN PAIGE, AND I KNOW FAUVE AND PAIGE DON'T GET ALONG.
"WE WERE WITH PAIGE."
OH, WHATEVER, DUDE. PAIGE LOOKED DESPERATE TO BE ANYWHERE ELSE.
YOU'RE NOT SUDDENLY ON THE SAME LEVEL AS PAIGE JUST BECAUSE YOU'RE BANGING HER COUSIN...
YOU SHUT THE FUCK UP, MICK!
YOU NEVER HEARD ME TALK ABOUT CHRISTIE LIKE THAT!

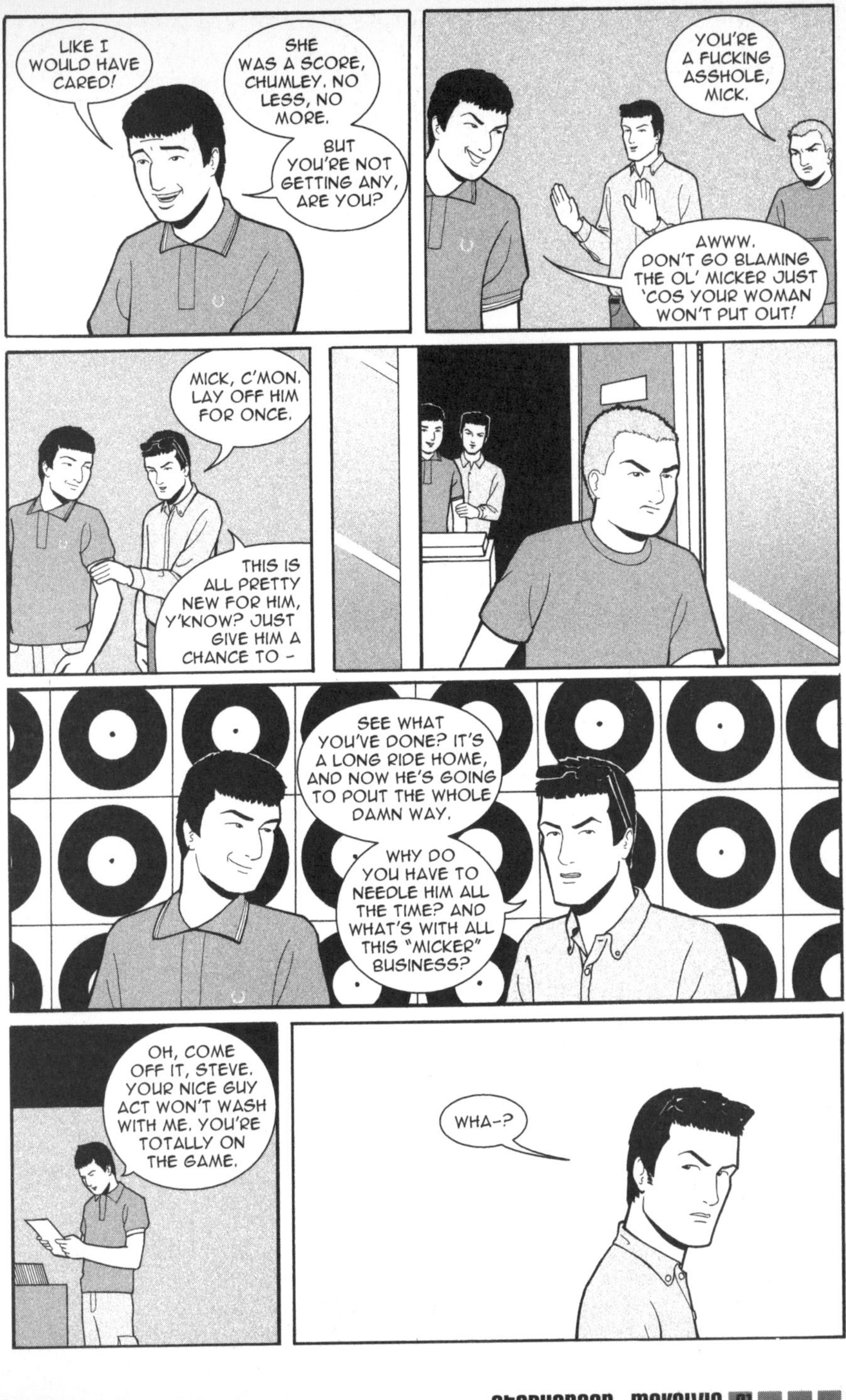
LIKE I WOULD HAVE CARED!
SHE WAS A SCORE, CHUMLEY. NO LESS, NO MORE.
BUT YOU'RE NOT GETTING ANY, ARE YOU?
YOU'RE A FUCKING ASSHOLE, MICK.
AWWW. DON'T GO BLAMING THE OL' MICKER JUST 'COS YOUR WOMAN WON'T PUT OUT!
MICK, C'MON. LAY OFF HIM FOR ONCE.
THIS IS ALL PRETTY NEW FOR HIM, Y'KNOW? JUST GIVE HIM A CHANCE TO -
SEE WHAT YOU'VE DONE? IT'S A LONG RIDE HOME, AND NOW HE'S GOING TO POUT THE WHOLE DAMN WAY.
WHY DO YOU HAVE TO NEEDLE HIM ALL THE TIME? AND WHAT'S WITH ALL THIS "MICKER" BUSINESS?
OH, COME OFF IT, STEVE. YOUR NICE GUY ACT WON'T WASH WITH ME. YOU'RE TOTALLY ON THE GAME.
WHA-?

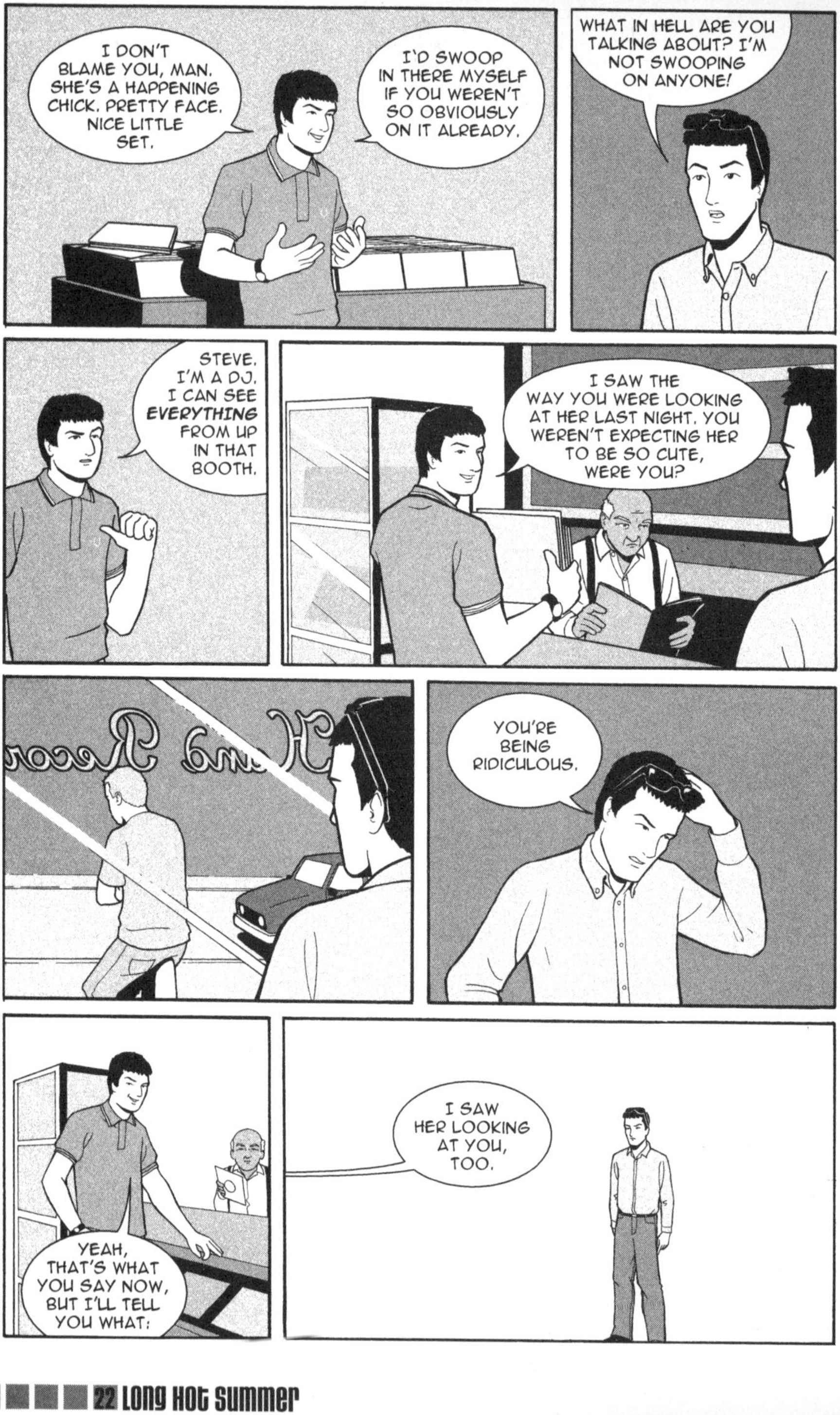
I DON'T BLAME YOU, MAN. SHE'S A HAPPENING CHICK. PRETTY FACE. NICE LITTLE SET.
I'D SWOOP IN THERE MYSELF IF YOU WEREN'T SO OBVIOUSLY ON IT ALREADY.
WHAT IN HELL ARE YOU TALKING ABOUT? I'M NOT SWOOPING ON ANYONE!
STEVE. I'M A DJ. I CAN SEE **EVERYTHING** FROM UP IN THAT BOOTH.
I SAW THE WAY YOU WERE LOOKING AT HER LAST NIGHT. YOU WEREN'T EXPECTING HER TO BE SO CUTE, WERE YOU?
YOU'RE BEING RIDICULOUS.
YEAH, THAT'S WHAT YOU SAY NOW, BUT I'LL TELL YOU WHAT:
I SAW HER LOOKING AT YOU, TOO.

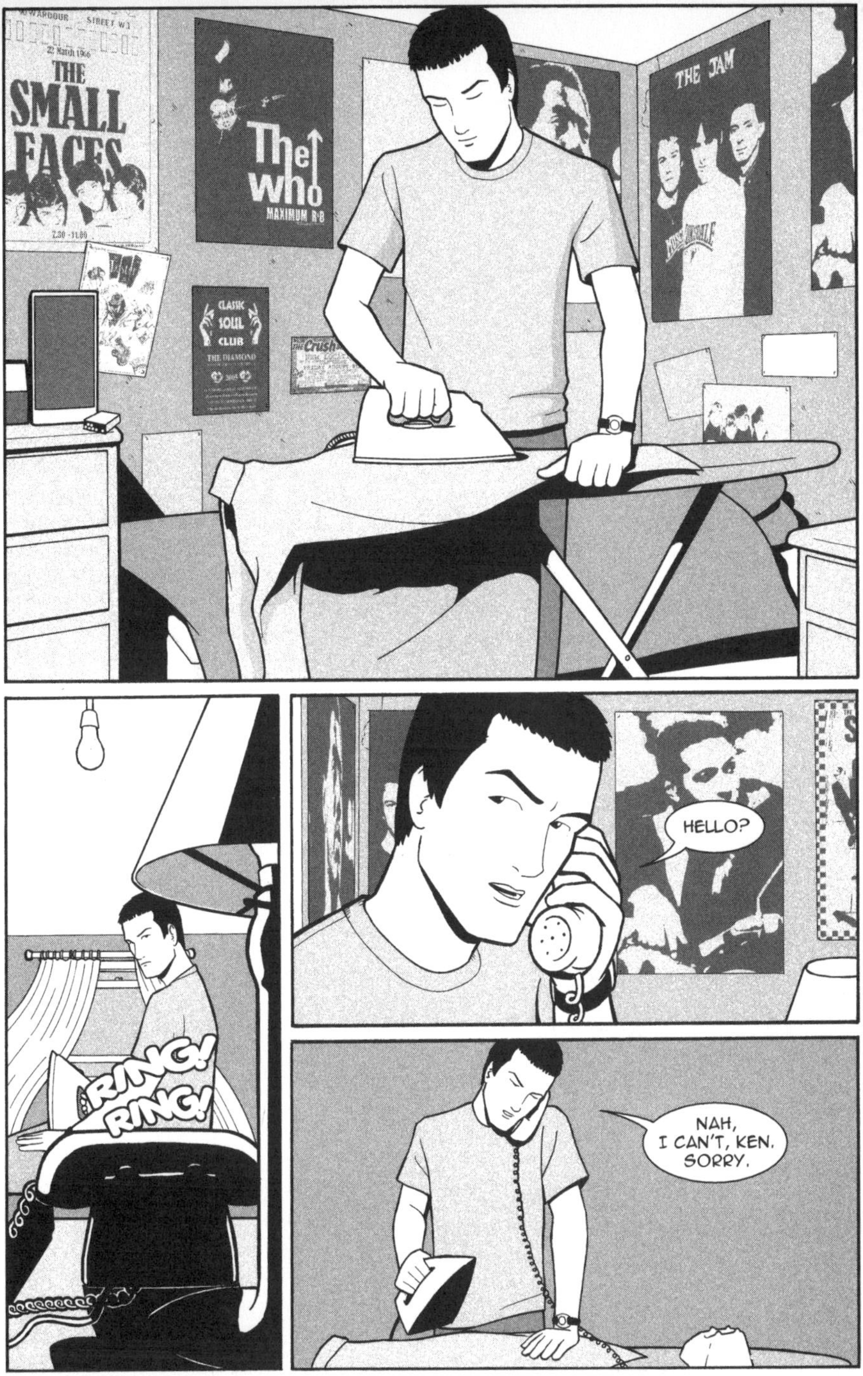
THE SMALL FACES
The Who
MAXIMUM R&B
THE JAM
CLASSIC SOUL CLUB
THE DIAMOND
RING!
RING!
HELLO?
NAH, I CAN'T, KEN. SORRY.

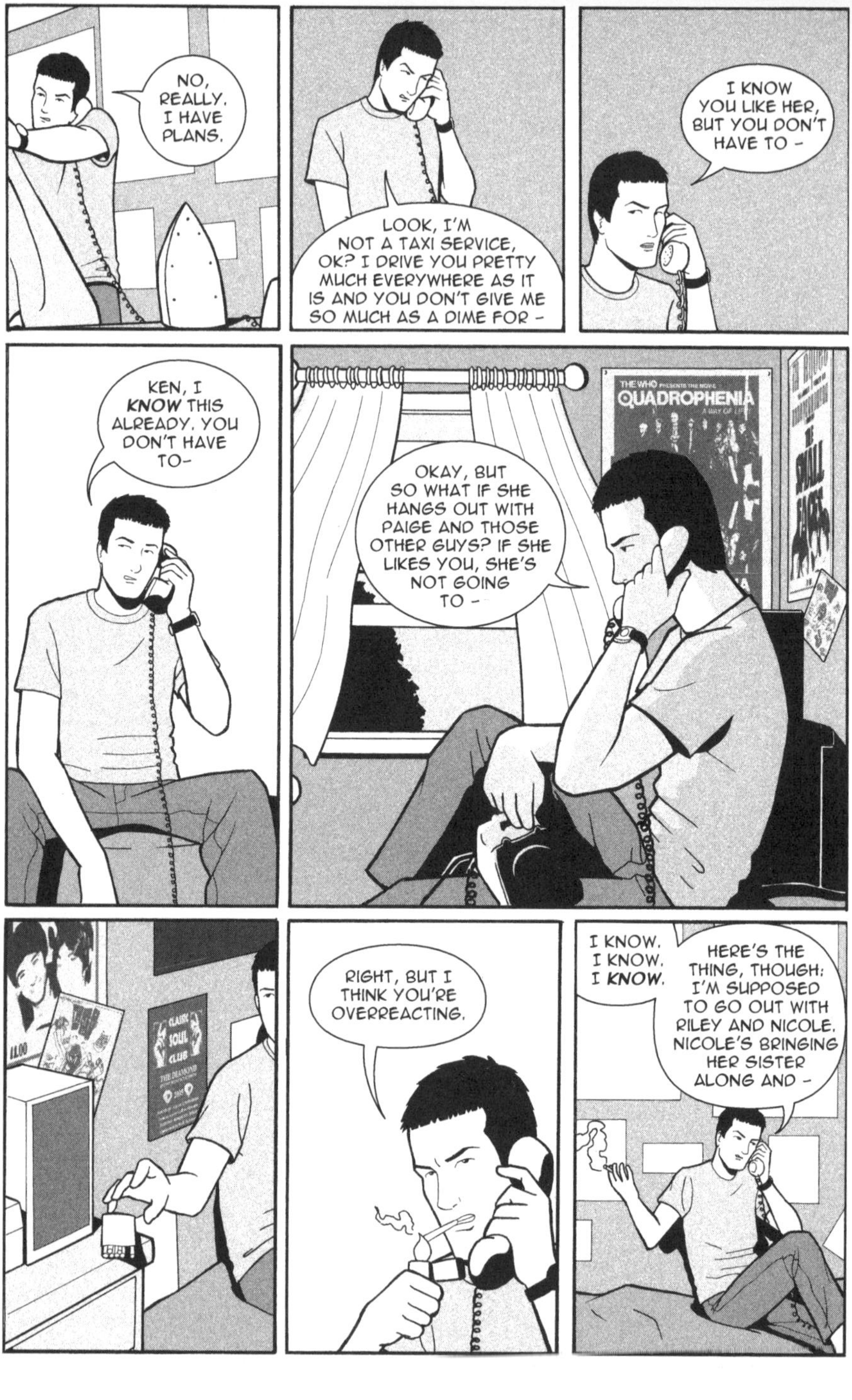
NO, REALLY. I HAVE PLANS.
LOOK, I'M NOT A TAXI SERVICE, OK? I DRIVE YOU PRETTY MUCH EVERYWHERE AS IT IS AND YOU DON'T GIVE ME SO MUCH AS A DIME FOR -
I KNOW YOU LIKE HER, BUT YOU DON'T HAVE TO -
KEN, I **KNOW** THIS ALREADY. YOU DON'T HAVE TO-
THE WHO PRESENTS THE MOVIE QUADROPHENIA
OKAY, BUT SO WHAT IF SHE HANGS OUT WITH PAIGE AND THOSE OTHER GUYS? IF SHE LIKES YOU, SHE'S NOT GOING TO -
RIGHT, BUT I THINK YOU'RE OVERREACTING.
I KNOW. I KNOW. I **KNOW**.
HERE'S THE THING, THOUGH: I'M SUPPOSED TO GO OUT WITH RILEY AND NICOLE. NICOLE'S BRINGING HER SISTER ALONG AND -

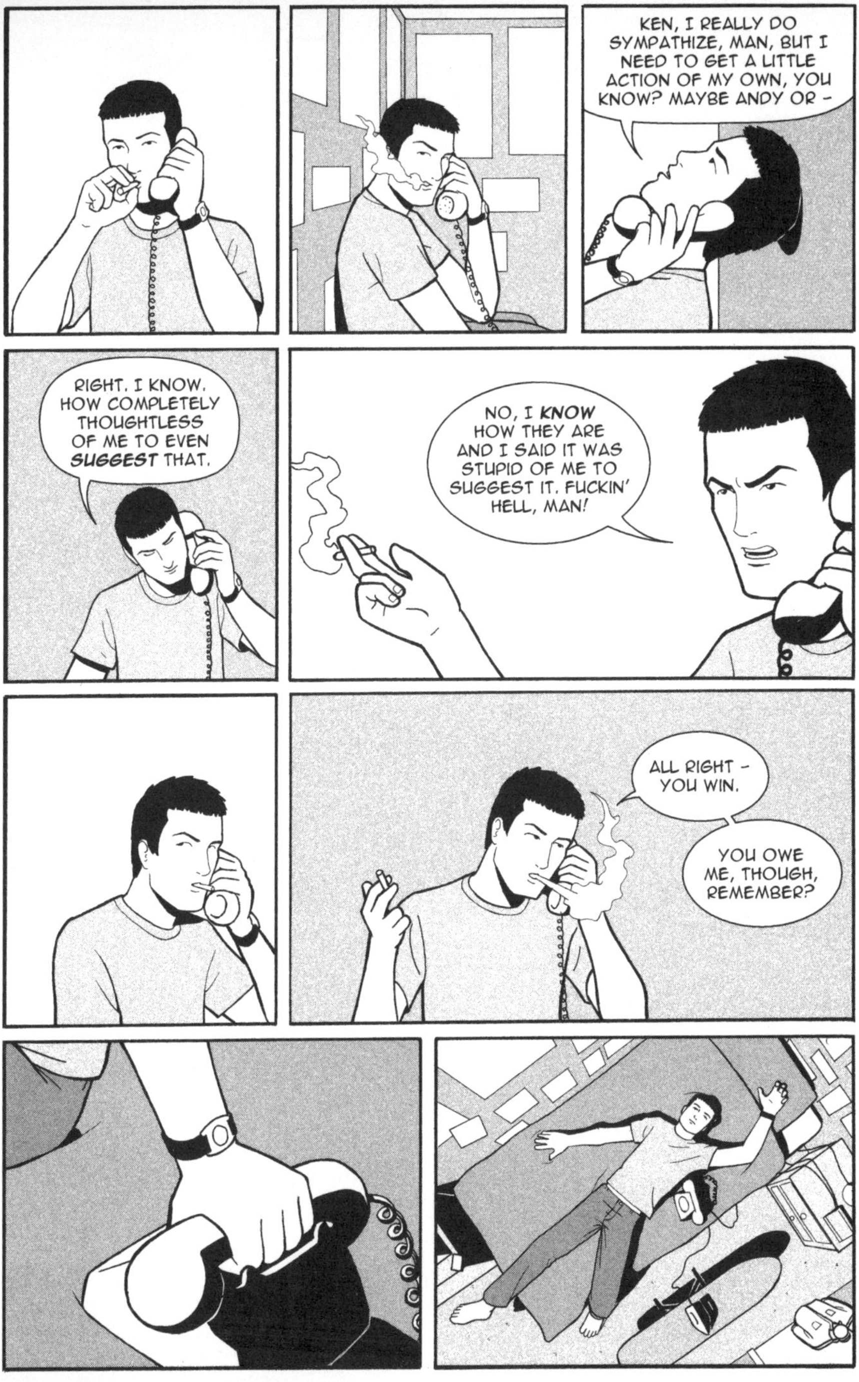
KEN, I REALLY DO SYMPATHIZE, MAN, BUT I NEED TO GET A LITTLE ACTION OF MY OWN, YOU KNOW? MAYBE ANDY OR -
RIGHT. I KNOW. HOW COMPLETELY THOUGHTLESS OF ME TO EVEN SUGGEST THAT.
NO, I KNOW HOW THEY ARE AND I SAID IT WAS STUPID OF ME TO SUGGEST IT. FUCKIN' HELL, MAN!
ALL RIGHT - YOU WIN.
YOU OWE ME, THOUGH, REMEMBER?

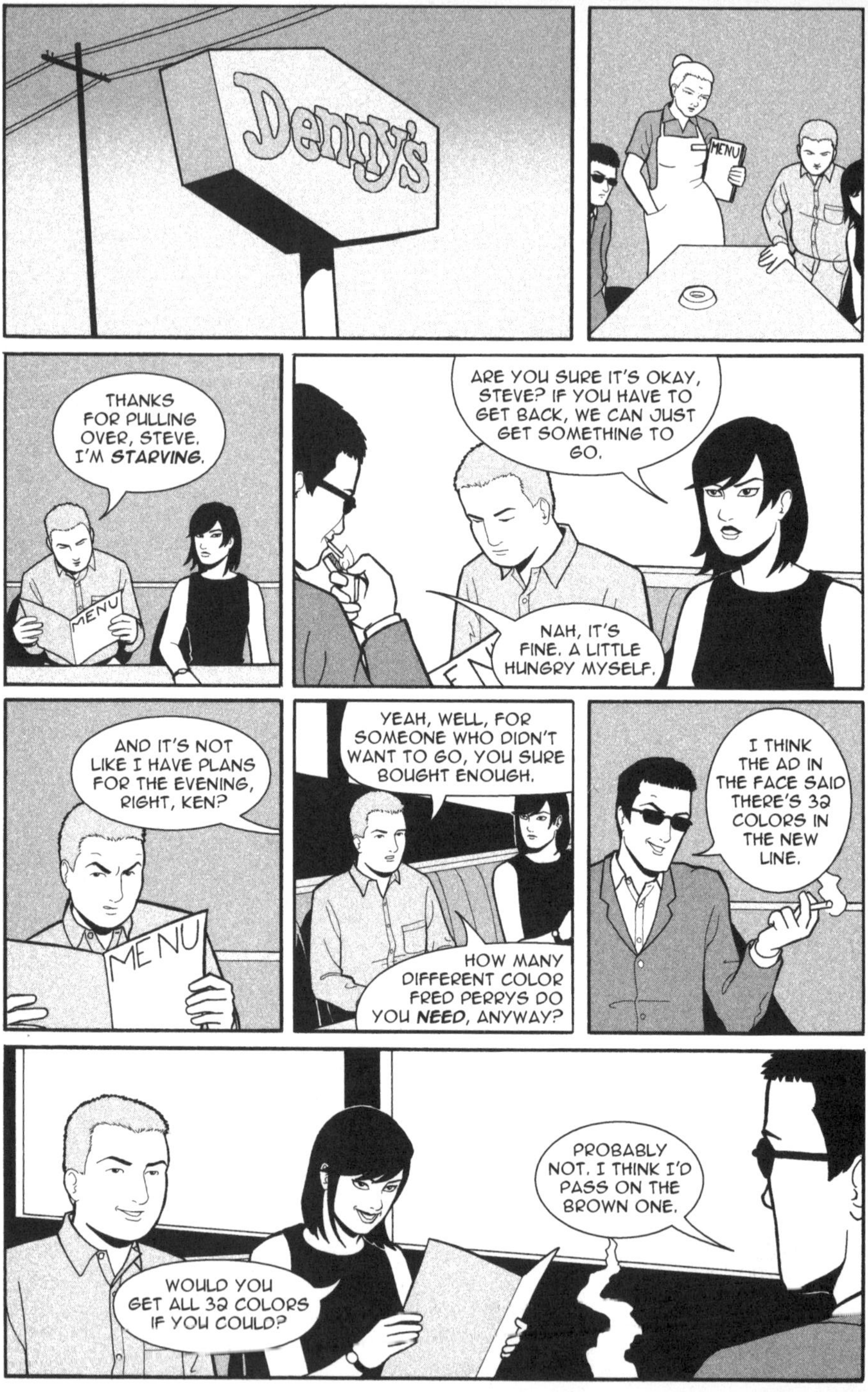
Denny's
MENU
THANKS FOR PULLING OVER, STEVE. I'M **STARVING**.
MENU
ARE YOU SURE IT'S OKAY, STEVE? IF YOU HAVE TO GET BACK, WE CAN JUST GET SOMETHING TO GO.
NAH, IT'S FINE. A LITTLE HUNGRY MYSELF.
AND IT'S NOT LIKE I HAVE PLANS FOR THE EVENING, RIGHT, KEN?
MENU
YEAH, WELL, FOR SOMEONE WHO DIDN'T WANT TO GO, YOU SURE BOUGHT ENOUGH.
HOW MANY DIFFERENT COLOR FRED PERRYS DO YOU **NEED**, ANYWAY?
I THINK THE AD IN THE FACE SAID THERE'S 32 COLORS IN THE NEW LINE.
PROBABLY NOT. I THINK I'D PASS ON THE BROWN ONE.
WOULD YOU GET ALL 32 COLORS IF YOU COULD?

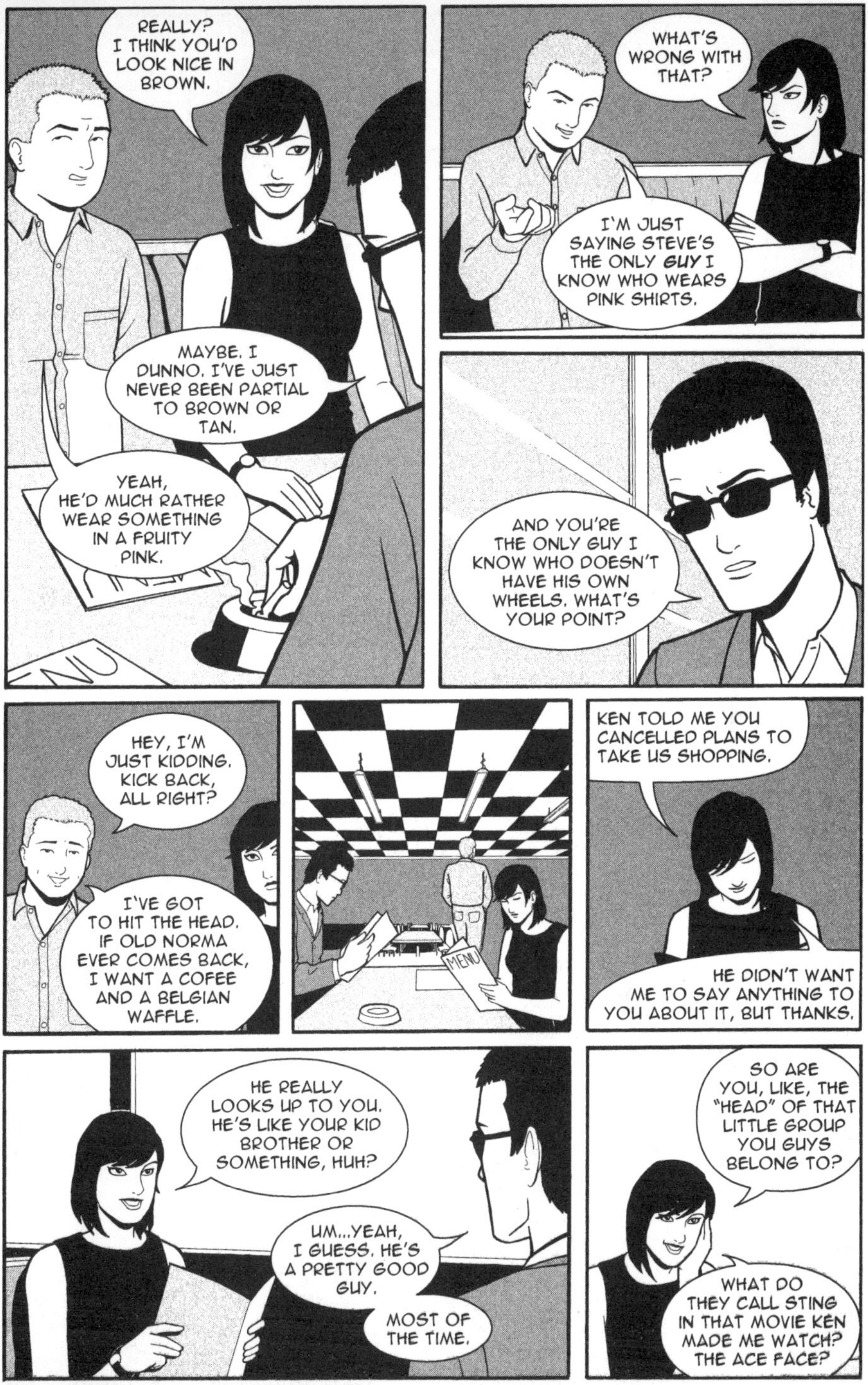
REALLY? I THINK YOU'D LOOK NICE IN BROWN.
MAYBE. I DUNNO. I'VE JUST NEVER BEEN PARTIAL TO BROWN OR TAN.
YEAH, HE'D MUCH RATHER WEAR SOMETHING IN A FRUITY PINK.
WHAT'S WRONG WITH THAT?
I'M JUST SAYING STEVE'S THE ONLY GUY I KNOW WHO WEARS PINK SHIRTS.
AND YOU'RE THE ONLY GUY I KNOW WHO DOESN'T HAVE HIS OWN WHEELS. WHAT'S YOUR POINT?
HEY, I'M JUST KIDDING. KICK BACK, ALL RIGHT?
I'VE GOT TO HIT THE HEAD. IF OLD NORMA EVER COMES BACK, I WANT A COFEE AND A BELGIAN WAFFLE.
MENU
KEN TOLD ME YOU CANCELLED PLANS TO TAKE US SHOPPING.
HE DIDN'T WANT ME TO SAY ANYTHING TO YOU ABOUT IT, BUT THANKS.
HE REALLY LOOKS UP TO YOU. HE'S LIKE YOUR KID BROTHER OR SOMETHING, HUH?
UM...YEAH, I GUESS. HE'S A PRETTY GOOD GUY.
MOST OF THE TIME.
SO ARE YOU, LIKE, THE "HEAD" OF THAT LITTLE GROUP YOU GUYS BELONG TO?
WHAT DO THEY CALL STING IN THAT MOVIE KEN MADE ME WATCH? THE ACE FACE?

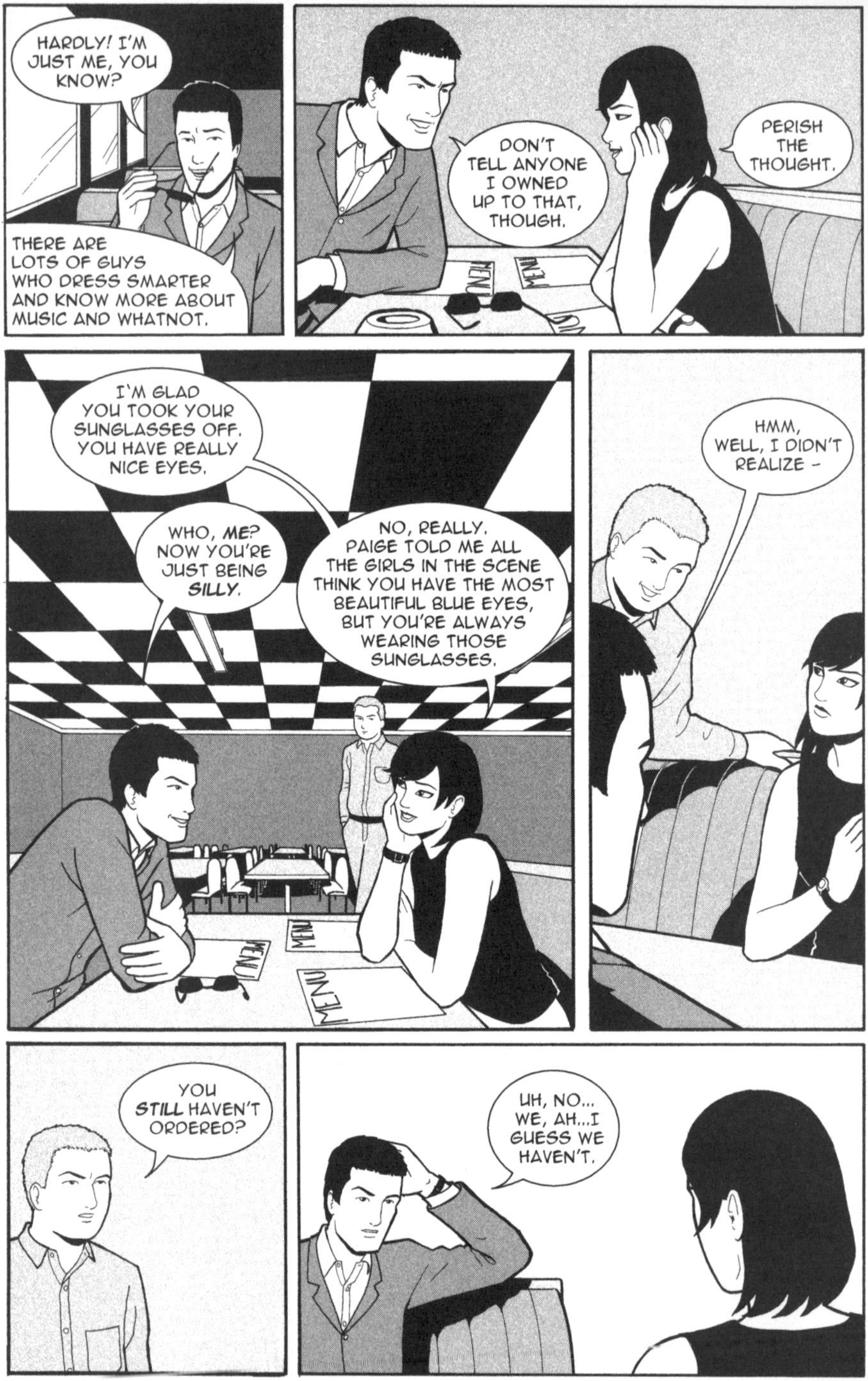
HARDLY! I'M JUST ME, YOU KNOW?
THERE ARE LOTS OF GUYS WHO DRESS SMARTER AND KNOW MORE ABOUT MUSIC AND WHATNOT.
DON'T TELL ANYONE I OWNED UP TO THAT, THOUGH.
PERISH THE THOUGHT.
MENU
MENU
I'M GLAD YOU TOOK YOUR SUNGLASSES OFF. YOU HAVE REALLY NICE EYES.
WHO, ME? NOW YOU'RE JUST BEING SILLY.
NO, REALLY. PAIGE TOLD ME ALL THE GIRLS IN THE SCENE THINK YOU HAVE THE MOST BEAUTIFUL BLUE EYES, BUT YOU'RE ALWAYS WEARING THOSE SUNGLASSES.
MENU
MENU
MENU
HMM, WELL, I DIDN'T REALIZE –
YOU STILL HAVEN'T ORDERED?
UH, NO... WE, AH...I GUESS WE HAVEN'T.

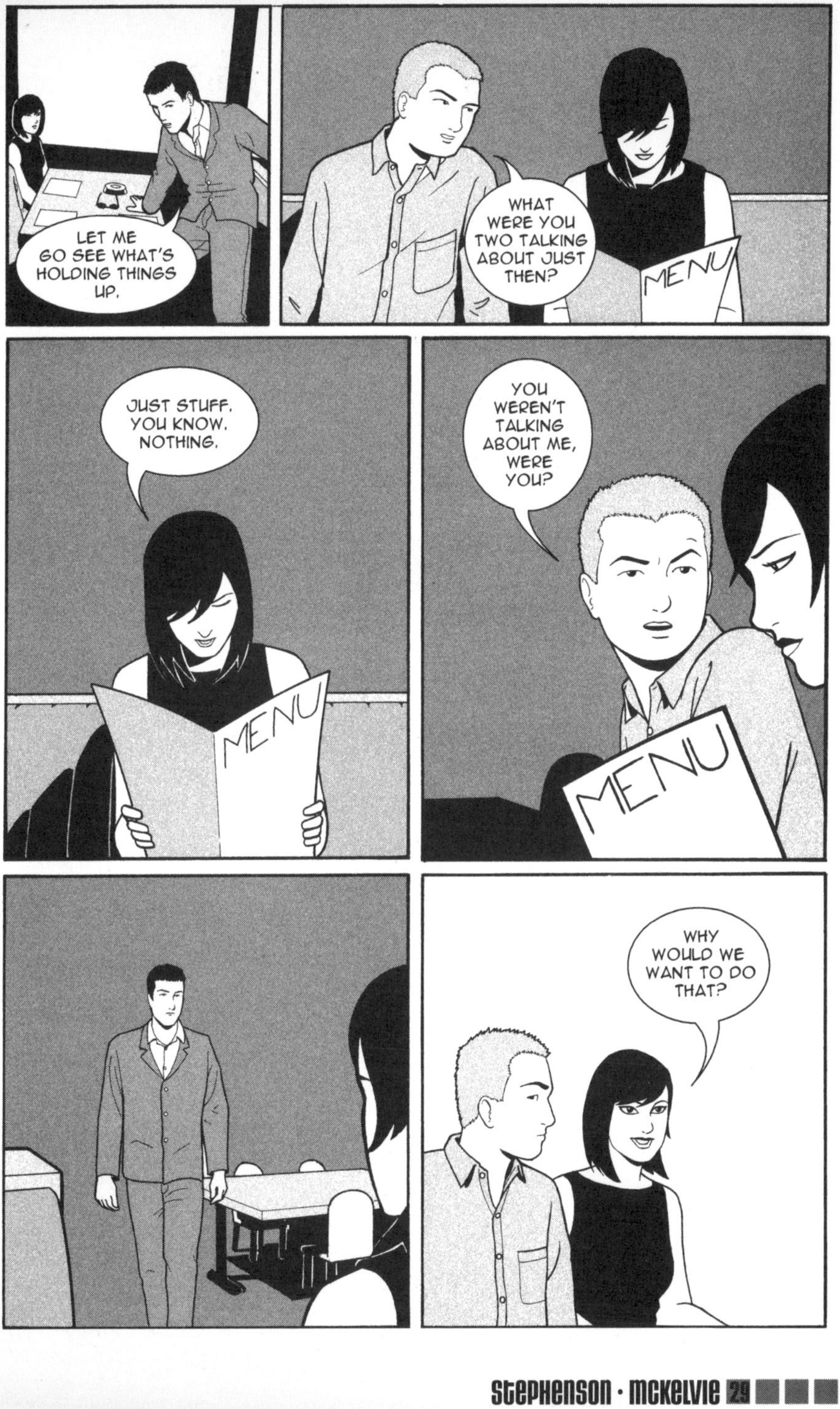

LET ME GO SEE WHAT'S HOLDING THINGS UP.
WHAT WERE YOU TWO TALKING ABOUT JUST THEN?
MENU
JUST STUFF. YOU KNOW. NOTHING.
MENU
YOU WEREN'T TALKING ABOUT ME, WERE YOU?
MENU
WHY WOULD WE WANT TO DO THAT?

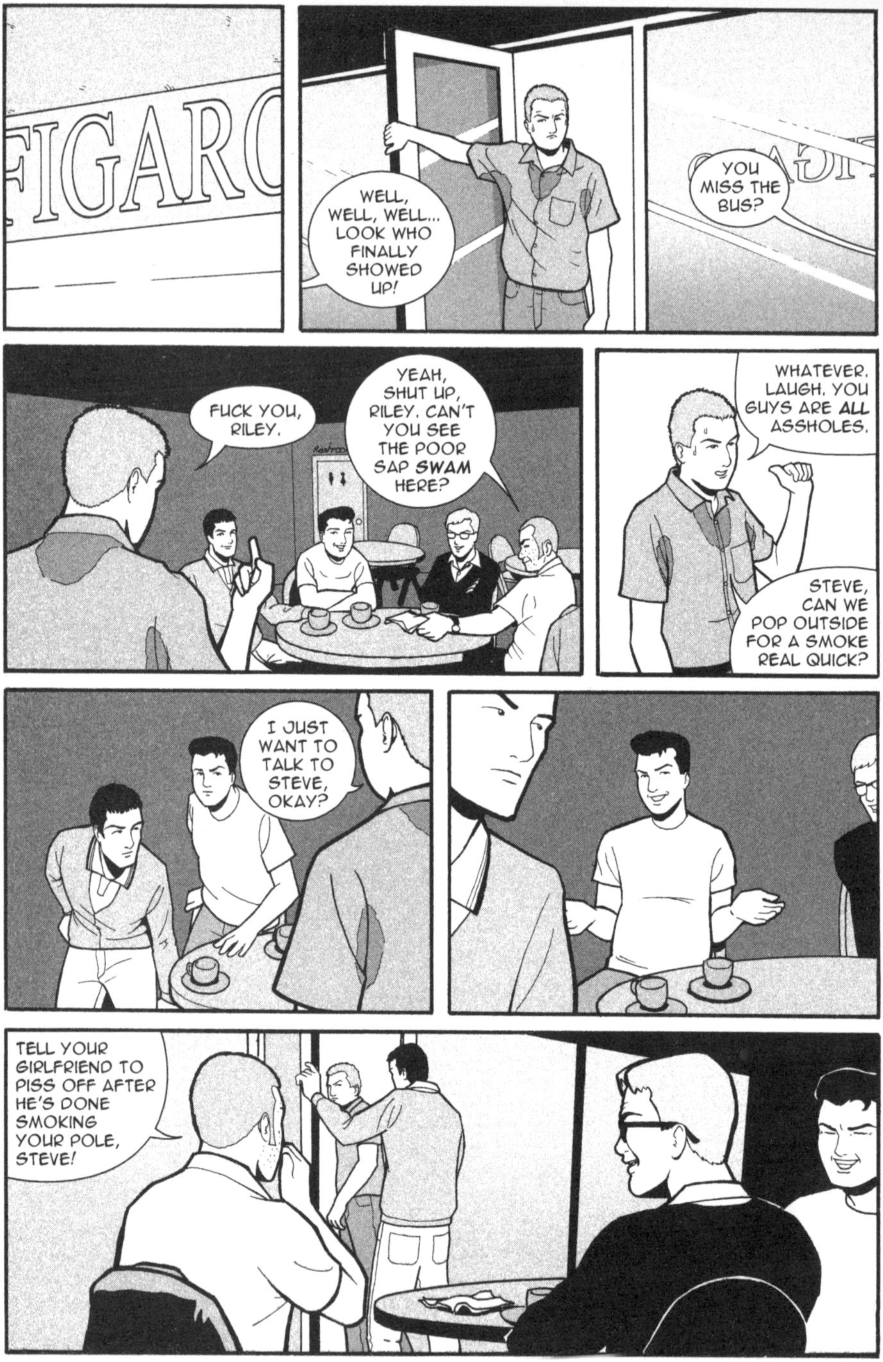
FIGARO
WELL, WELL, WELL... LOOK WHO FINALLY SHOWED UP!
YOU MISS THE BUS?
FUCK YOU, RILEY.
YEAH, SHUT UP, RILEY. CAN'T YOU SEE THE POOR SAP **SWAM** HERE?
WHATEVER. LAUGH. YOU GUYS ARE **ALL** ASSHOLES.
STEVE, CAN WE POP OUTSIDE FOR A SMOKE REAL QUICK?
I JUST WANT TO TALK TO STEVE, OKAY?
TELL YOUR GIRLFRIEND TO PISS OFF AFTER HE'S DONE SMOKING YOUR POLE, STEVE!

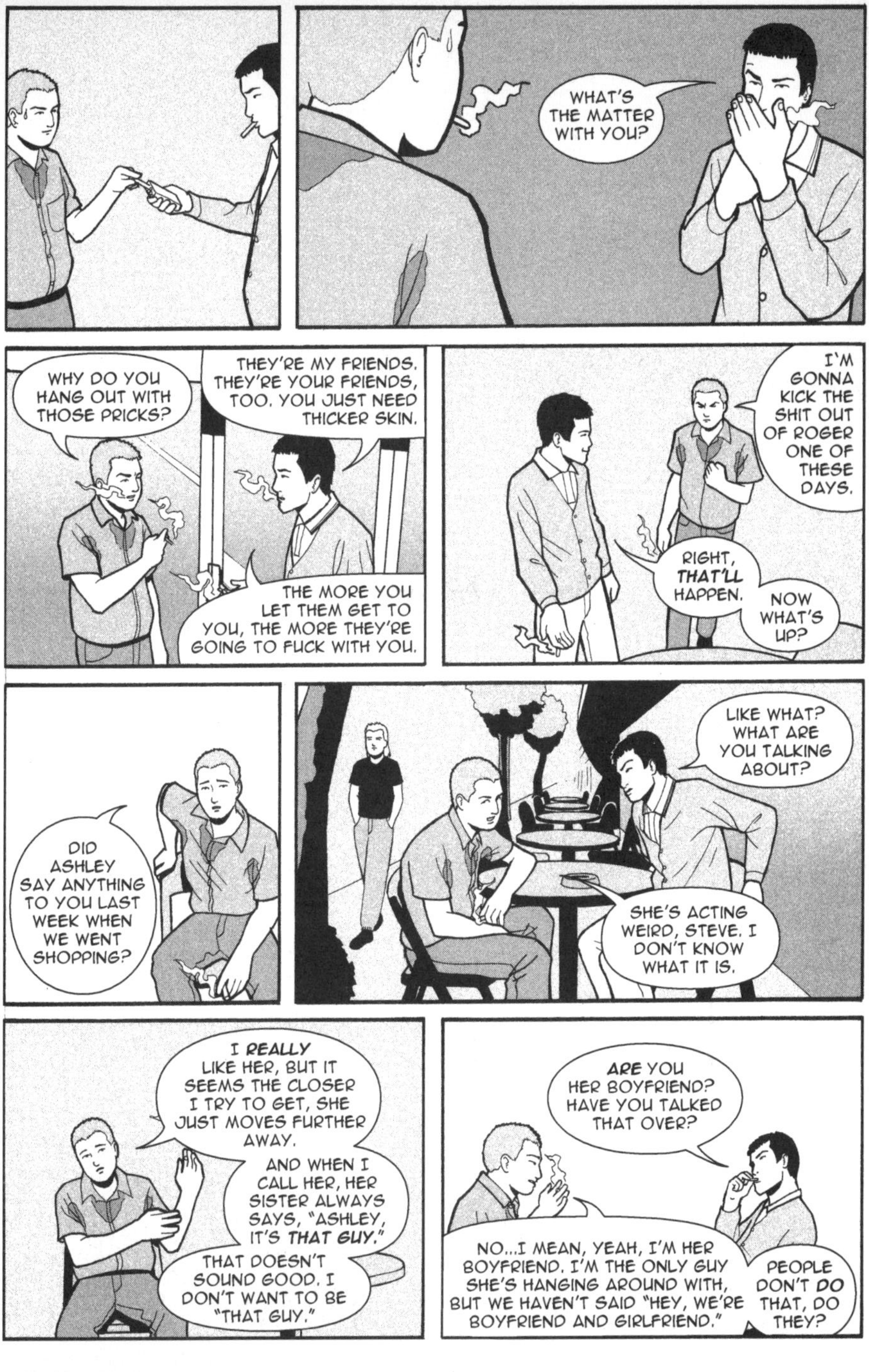
WHAT'S THE MATTER WITH YOU?
WHY DO YOU HANG OUT WITH THOSE PRICKS?
THEY'RE MY FRIENDS. THEY'RE YOUR FRIENDS, TOO. YOU JUST NEED THICKER SKIN.
THE MORE YOU LET THEM GET TO YOU, THE MORE THEY'RE GOING TO FUCK WITH YOU.
I'M GONNA KICK THE SHIT OUT OF ROGER ONE OF THESE DAYS.
RIGHT, THAT'LL HAPPEN.
NOW WHAT'S UP?
DID ASHLEY SAY ANYTHING TO YOU LAST WEEK WHEN WE WENT SHOPPING?
LIKE WHAT? WHAT ARE YOU TALKING ABOUT?
SHE'S ACTING WEIRD, STEVE. I DON'T KNOW WHAT IT IS.
I REALLY LIKE HER, BUT IT SEEMS THE CLOSER I TRY TO GET, SHE JUST MOVES FURTHER AWAY.
AND WHEN I CALL HER, HER SISTER ALWAYS SAYS, "ASHLEY, IT'S THAT GUY."
THAT DOESN'T SOUND GOOD. I DON'T WANT TO BE "THAT GUY."
ARE YOU HER BOYFRIEND? HAVE YOU TALKED THAT OVER?
NO...I MEAN, YEAH, I'M HER BOYFRIEND. I'M THE ONLY GUY SHE'S HANGING AROUND WITH, BUT WE HAVEN'T SAID "HEY, WE'RE BOYFRIEND AND GIRLFRIEND."
PEOPLE DON'T DO THAT, DO THEY?

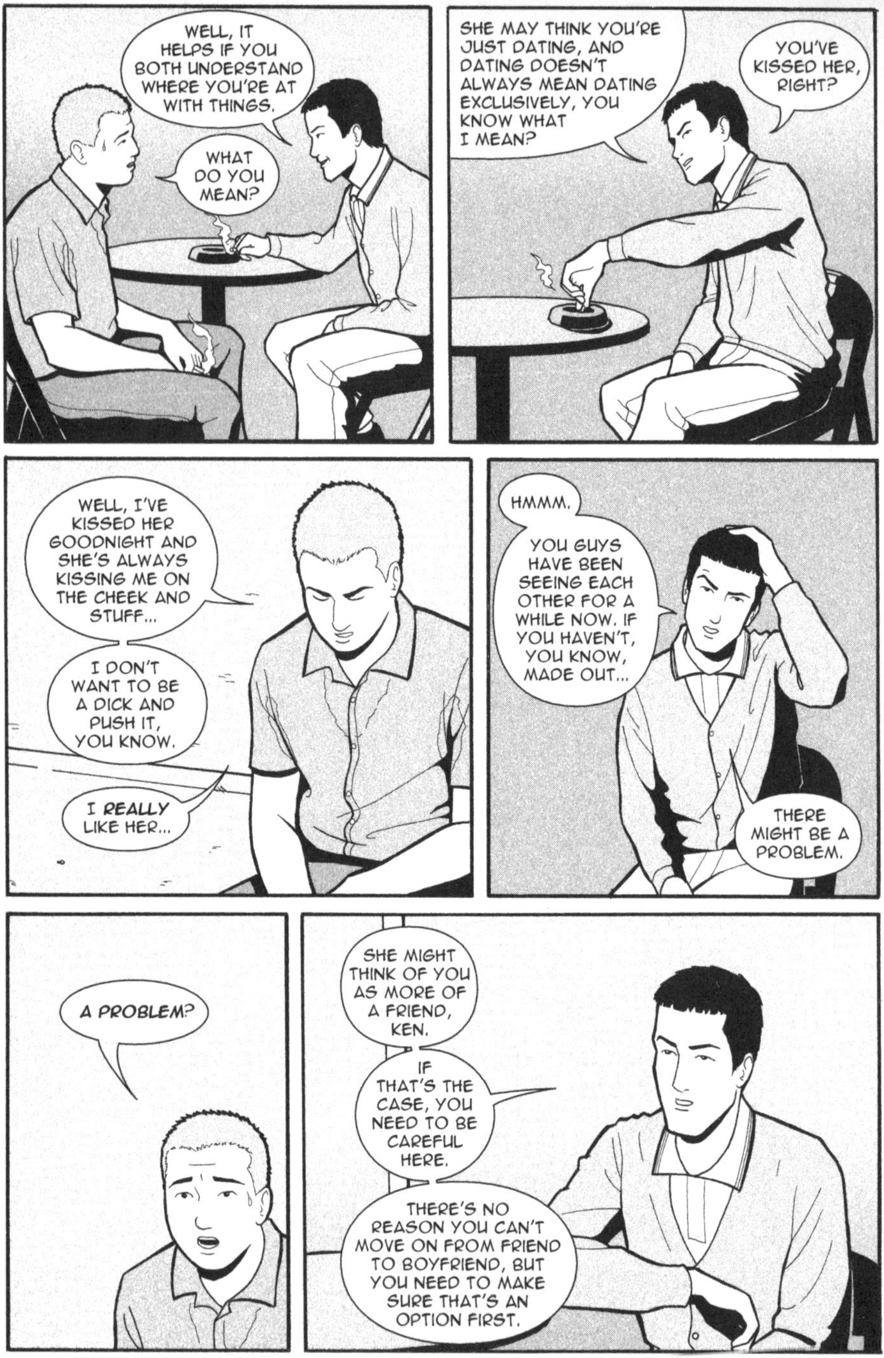
WELL, IT HELPS IF YOU BOTH UNDERSTAND WHERE YOU'RE AT WITH THINGS.
WHAT DO YOU MEAN?
SHE MAY THINK YOU'RE JUST DATING, AND DATING DOESN'T ALWAYS MEAN DATING EXCLUSIVELY, YOU KNOW WHAT I MEAN?
YOU'VE KISSED HER, RIGHT?
WELL, I'VE KISSED HER GOODNIGHT AND SHE'S ALWAYS KISSING ME ON THE CHEEK AND STUFF...
I DON'T WANT TO BE A DICK AND PUSH IT, YOU KNOW.
I *REALLY* LIKE HER...
HMMM.
YOU GUYS HAVE BEEN SEEING EACH OTHER FOR A WHILE NOW. IF YOU HAVEN'T, YOU KNOW, MADE OUT...
THERE MIGHT BE A PROBLEM.
A PROBLEM?
SHE MIGHT THINK OF YOU AS MORE OF A FRIEND, KEN.
IF THAT'S THE CASE, YOU NEED TO BE CAREFUL HERE.
THERE'S NO REASON YOU CAN'T MOVE ON FROM FRIEND TO BOYFRIEND, BUT YOU NEED TO MAKE SURE THAT'S AN OPTION FIRST.

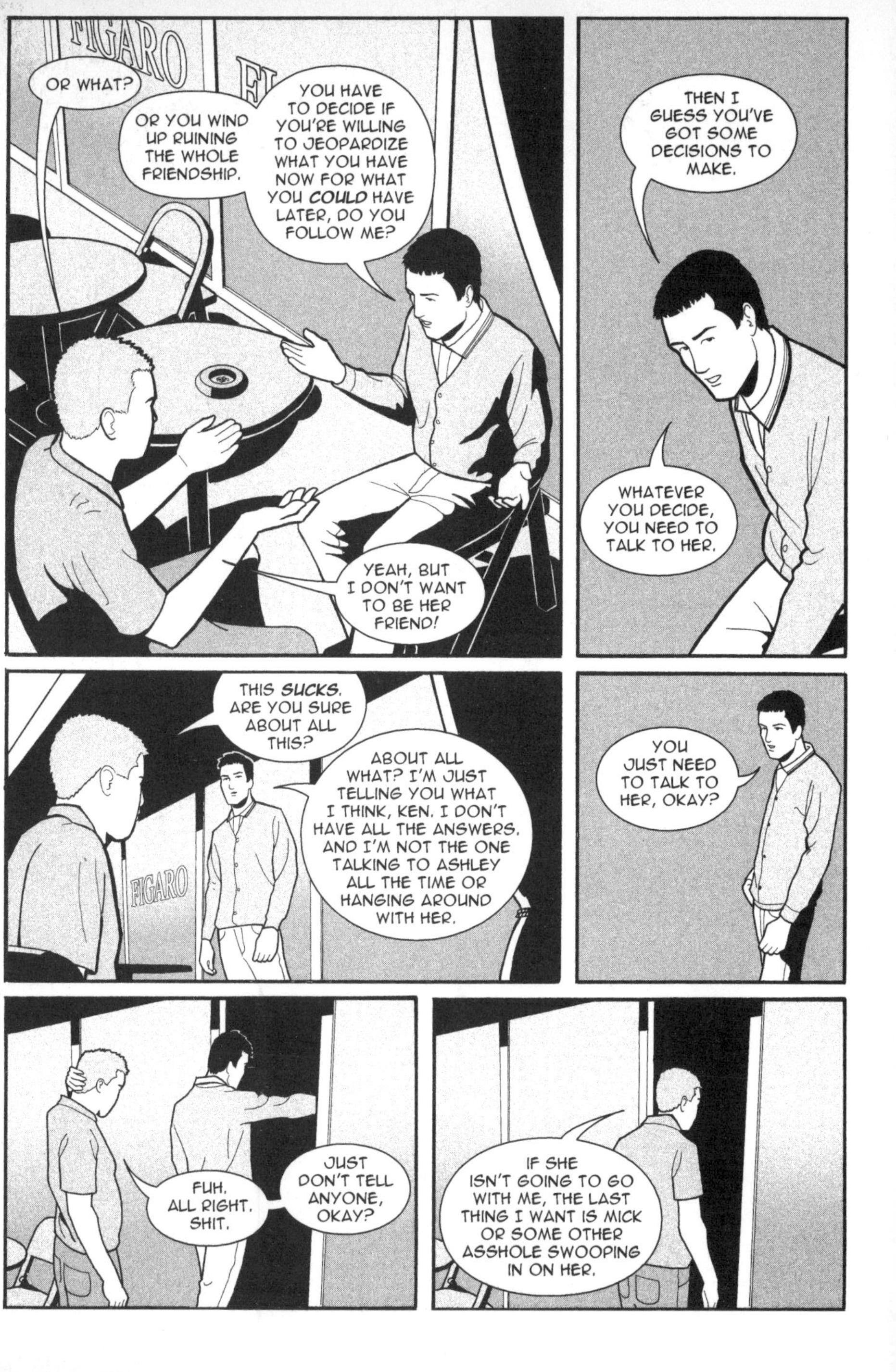
FIGARO
OR WHAT?
OR YOU WIND UP RUINING THE WHOLE FRIENDSHIP.
YOU HAVE TO DECIDE IF YOU'RE WILLING TO JEOPARDIZE WHAT YOU HAVE NOW FOR WHAT YOU COULD HAVE LATER, DO YOU FOLLOW ME?
YEAH, BUT I DON'T WANT TO BE HER FRIEND!
THEN I GUESS YOU'VE GOT SOME DECISIONS TO MAKE.
WHATEVER YOU DECIDE, YOU NEED TO TALK TO HER.
THIS SUCKS. ARE YOU SURE ABOUT ALL THIS?
ABOUT ALL WHAT? I'M JUST TELLING YOU WHAT I THINK, KEN. I DON'T HAVE ALL THE ANSWERS, AND I'M NOT THE ONE TALKING TO ASHLEY ALL THE TIME OR HANGING AROUND WITH HER.
FIGARO
YOU JUST NEED TO TALK TO HER, OKAY?
FUH. ALL RIGHT. SHIT.
JUST DON'T TELL ANYONE, OKAY?
IF SHE ISN'T GOING TO GO WITH ME, THE LAST THING I WANT IS MICK OR SOME OTHER ASSHOLE SWOOPING IN ON HER.

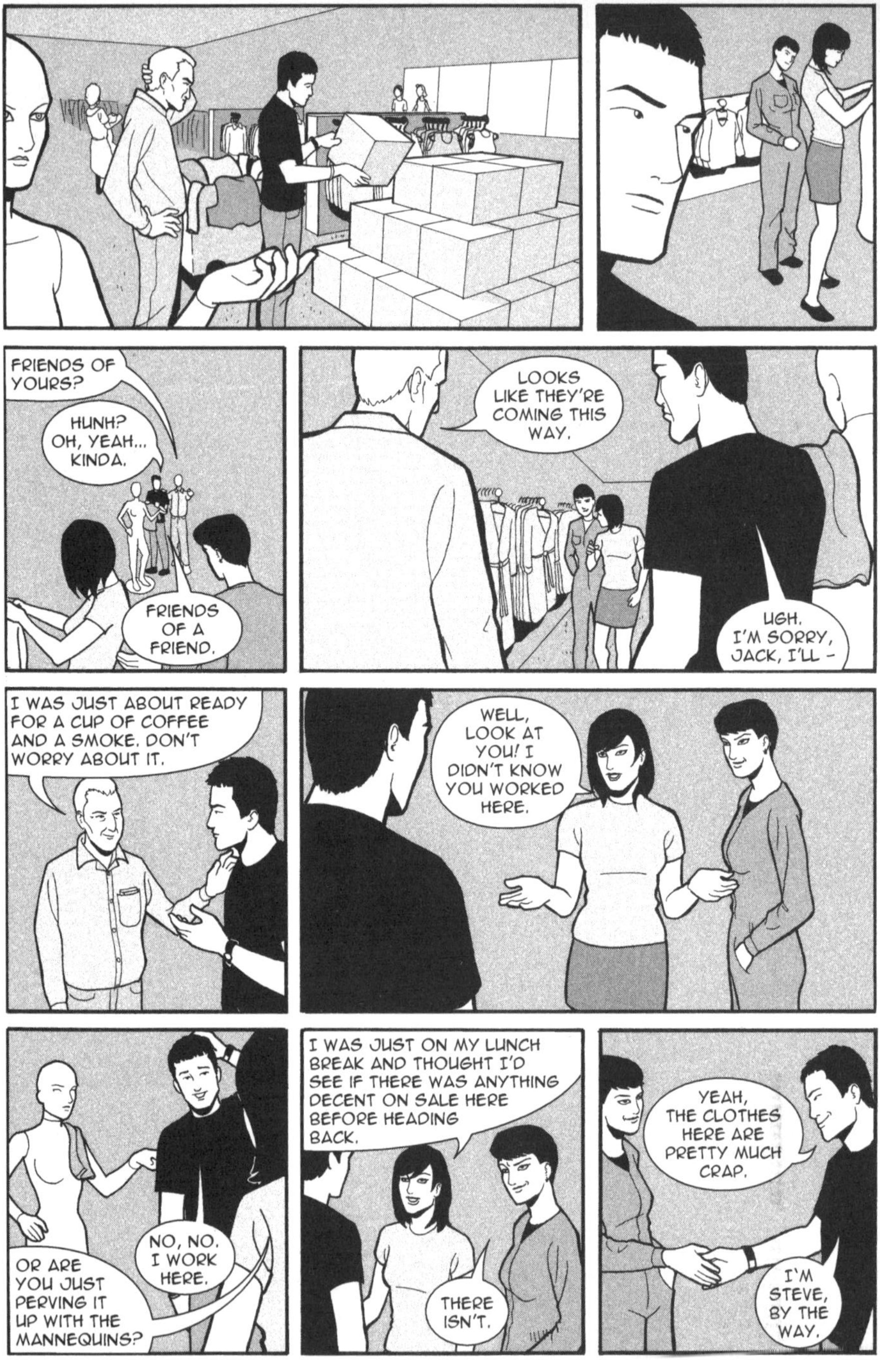
FRIENDS OF YOURS?
HUNH? OH, YEAH... KINDA.
FRIENDS OF A FRIEND.
LOOKS LIKE THEY'RE COMING THIS WAY.
UGH. I'M SORRY, JACK, I'LL -
I WAS JUST ABOUT READY FOR A CUP OF COFFEE AND A SMOKE. DON'T WORRY ABOUT IT.
WELL, LOOK AT YOU! I DIDN'T KNOW YOU WORKED HERE.
OR ARE YOU JUST PERVING IT UP WITH THE MANNEQUINS?
NO, NO. I WORK HERE.
I WAS JUST ON MY LUNCH BREAK AND THOUGHT I'D SEE IF THERE WAS ANYTHING DECENT ON SALE HERE BEFORE HEADING BACK.
THERE ISN'T.
YEAH, THE CLOTHES HERE ARE PRETTY MUCH CRAP.
I'M STEVE, BY THE WAY.

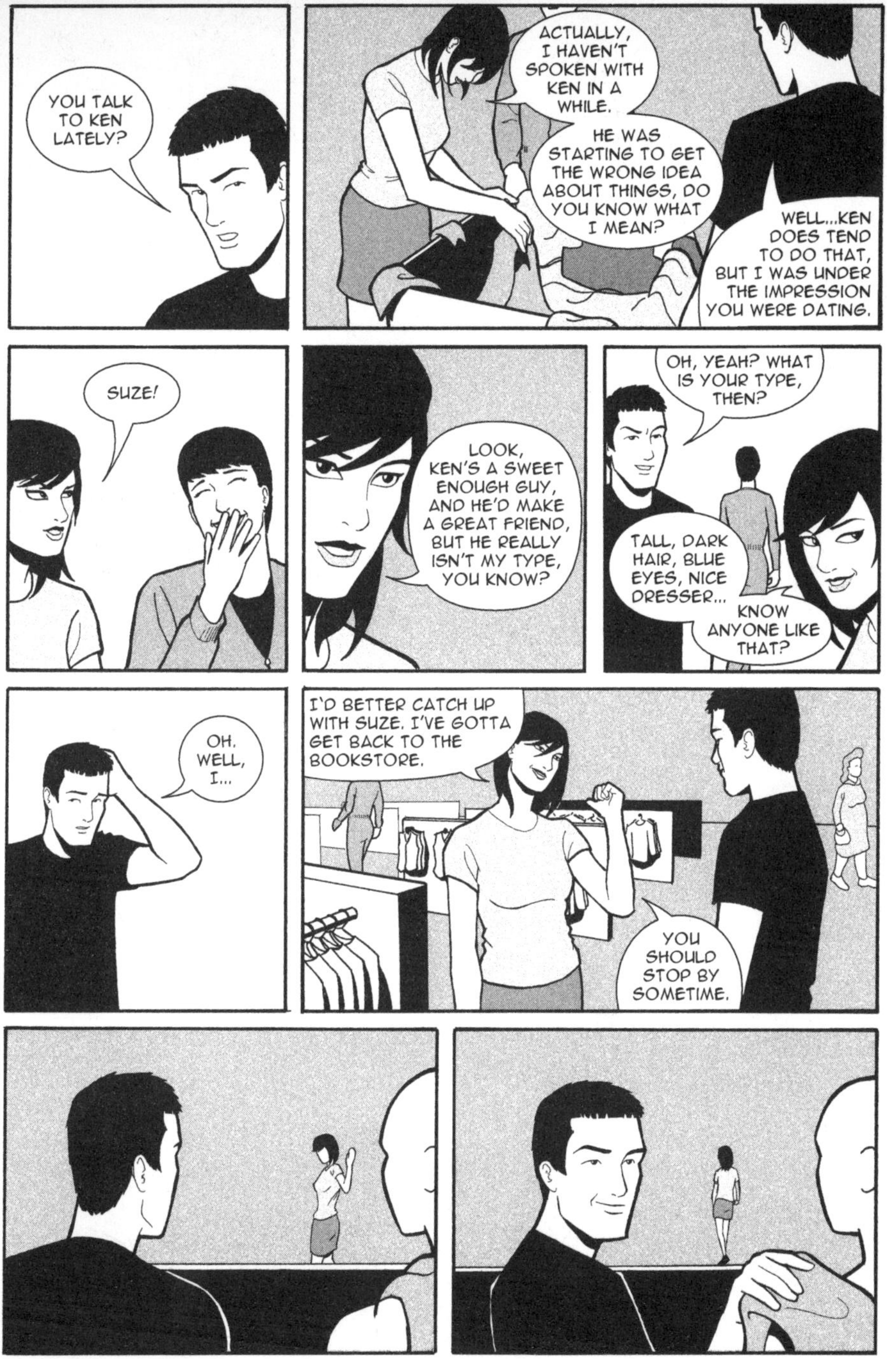

YOU TALK TO KEN LATELY?
ACTUALLY, I HAVEN'T SPOKEN WITH KEN IN A WHILE.
HE WAS STARTING TO GET THE WRONG IDEA ABOUT THINGS, DO YOU KNOW WHAT I MEAN?
WELL...KEN DOES TEND TO DO THAT, BUT I WAS UNDER THE IMPRESSION YOU WERE DATING.
SUZE!
LOOK, KEN'S A SWEET ENOUGH GUY, AND HE'D MAKE A GREAT FRIEND, BUT HE REALLY ISN'T MY TYPE, YOU KNOW?
OH, YEAH? WHAT IS YOUR TYPE, THEN?
TALL, DARK HAIR, BLUE EYES, NICE DRESSER...
KNOW ANYONE LIKE THAT?
OH. WELL, I...
I'D BETTER CATCH UP WITH SUZE. I'VE GOTTA GET BACK TO THE BOOKSTORE.
YOU SHOULD STOP BY SOMETIME.

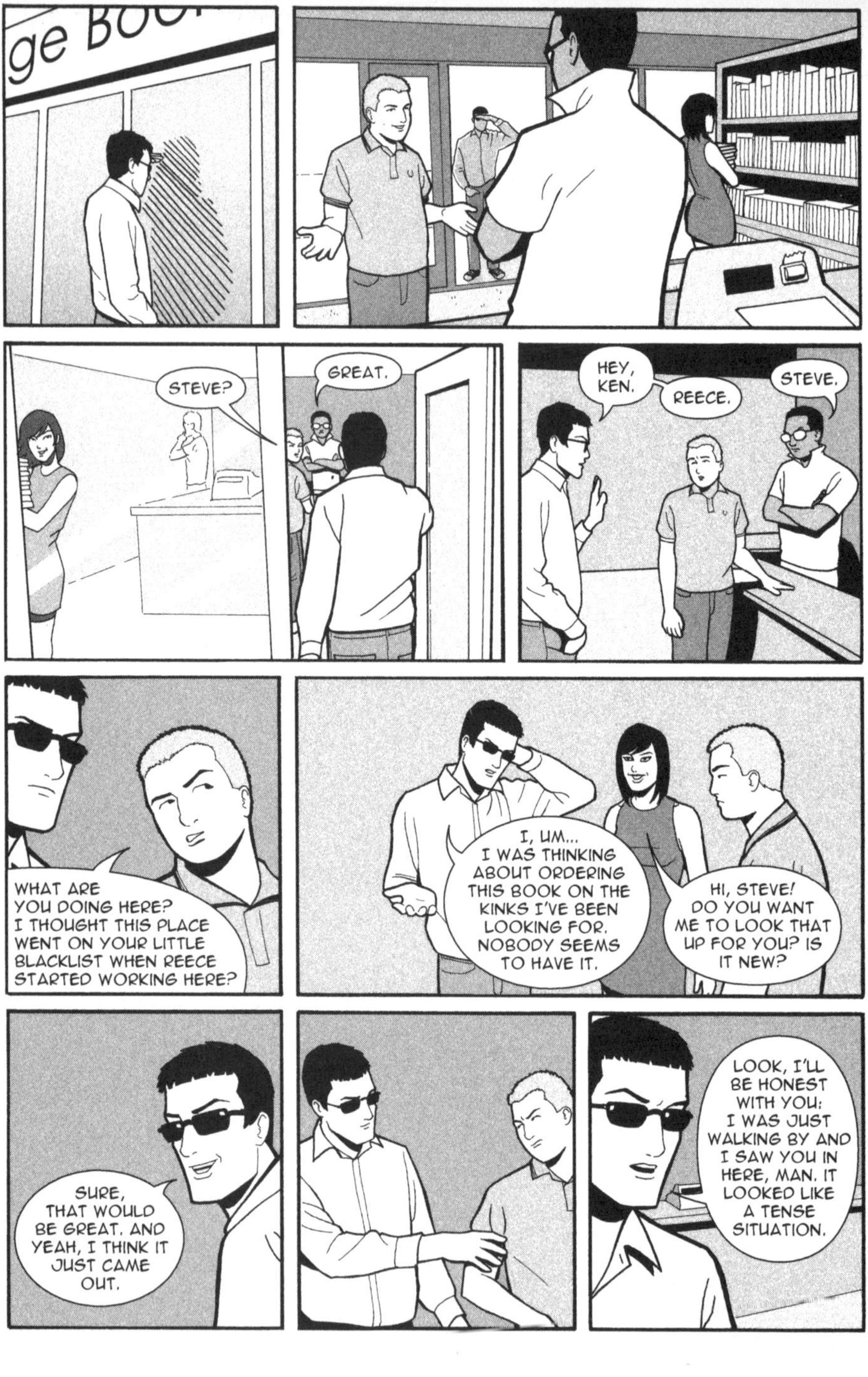
ge BOO
STEVE?
GREAT.
HEY, KEN.
REECE.
STEVE.
WHAT ARE YOU DOING HERE? I THOUGHT THIS PLACE WENT ON YOUR LITTLE BLACKLIST WHEN REECE STARTED WORKING HERE?
I, UM... I WAS THINKING ABOUT ORDERING THIS BOOK ON THE KINKS I'VE BEEN LOOKING FOR. NOBODY SEEMS TO HAVE IT.
HI, STEVE! DO YOU WANT ME TO LOOK THAT UP FOR YOU? IS IT NEW?
SURE, THAT WOULD BE GREAT. AND YEAH, I THINK IT JUST CAME OUT.
LOOK, I'LL BE HONEST WITH YOU: I WAS JUST WALKING BY AND I SAW YOU IN HERE, MAN. IT LOOKED LIKE A TENSE SITUATION.

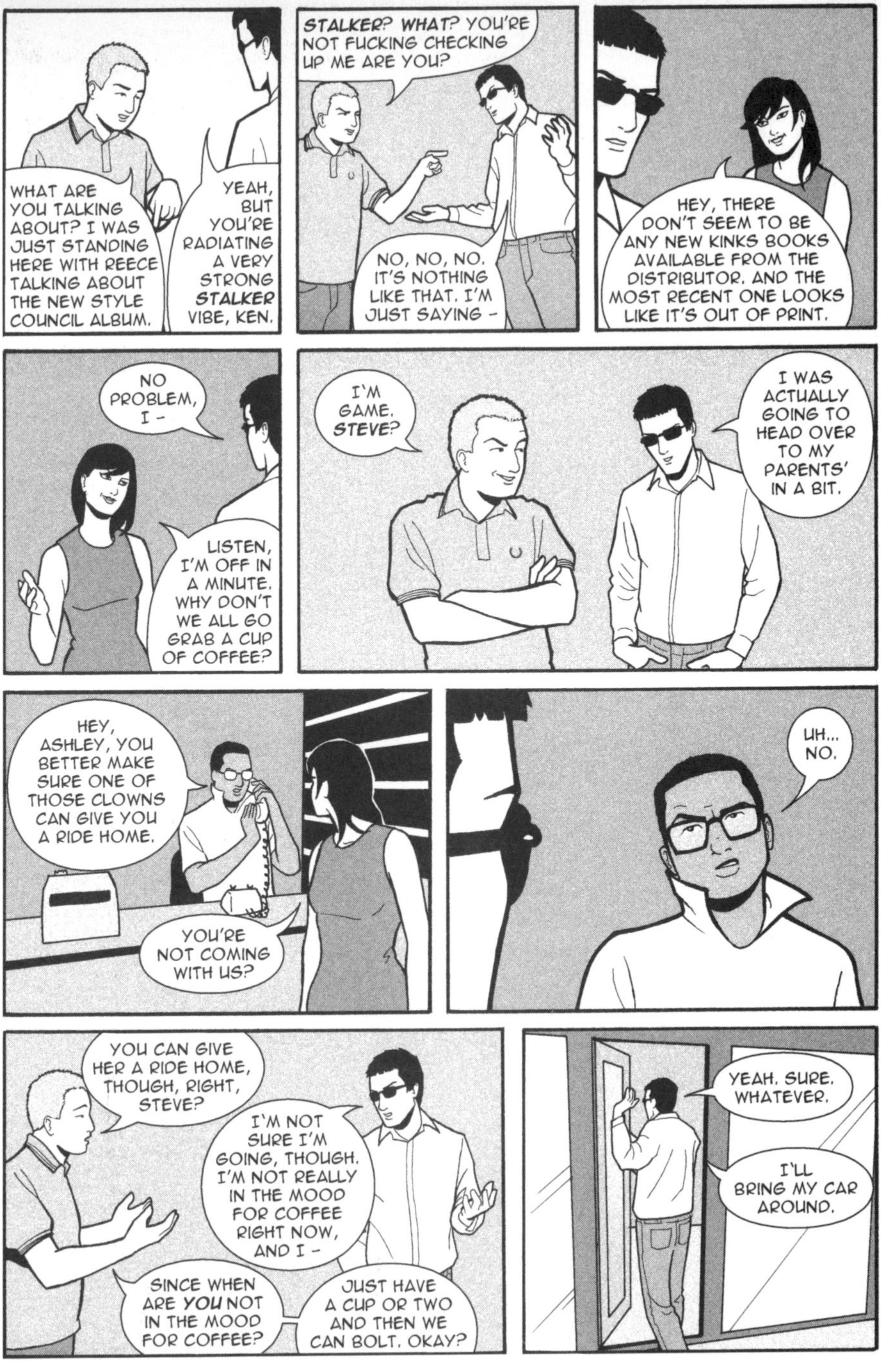
WHAT ARE YOU TALKING ABOUT? I WAS JUST STANDING HERE WITH REECE TALKING ABOUT THE NEW STYLE COUNCIL ALBUM.
YEAH, BUT YOU'RE RADIATING A VERY STRONG **STALKER** VIBE, KEN.
STALKER? WHAT? YOU'RE NOT FUCKING CHECKING UP ME ARE YOU?
NO, NO, NO. IT'S NOTHING LIKE THAT. I'M JUST SAYING –
HEY, THERE DON'T SEEM TO BE ANY NEW KINKS BOOKS AVAILABLE FROM THE DISTRIBUTOR. AND THE MOST RECENT ONE LOOKS LIKE IT'S OUT OF PRINT.
NO PROBLEM, I –
LISTEN, I'M OFF IN A MINUTE. WHY DON'T WE ALL GO GRAB A CUP OF COFFEE?
I'M GAME. **STEVE?**
I WAS ACTUALLY GOING TO HEAD OVER TO MY PARENTS' IN A BIT.
HEY, ASHLEY, YOU BETTER MAKE SURE ONE OF THOSE CLOWNS CAN GIVE YOU A RIDE HOME.
YOU'RE NOT COMING WITH US?
UH... NO.
YOU CAN GIVE HER A RIDE HOME, THOUGH, RIGHT, STEVE?
I'M NOT SURE I'M GOING, THOUGH. I'M NOT REALLY IN THE MOOD FOR COFFEE RIGHT NOW, AND I –
SINCE WHEN ARE **YOU** NOT IN THE MOOD FOR COFFEE?
JUST HAVE A CUP OR TWO AND THEN WE CAN BOLT. OKAY?
YEAH. SURE. WHATEVER.
I'LL BRING MY CAR AROUND.

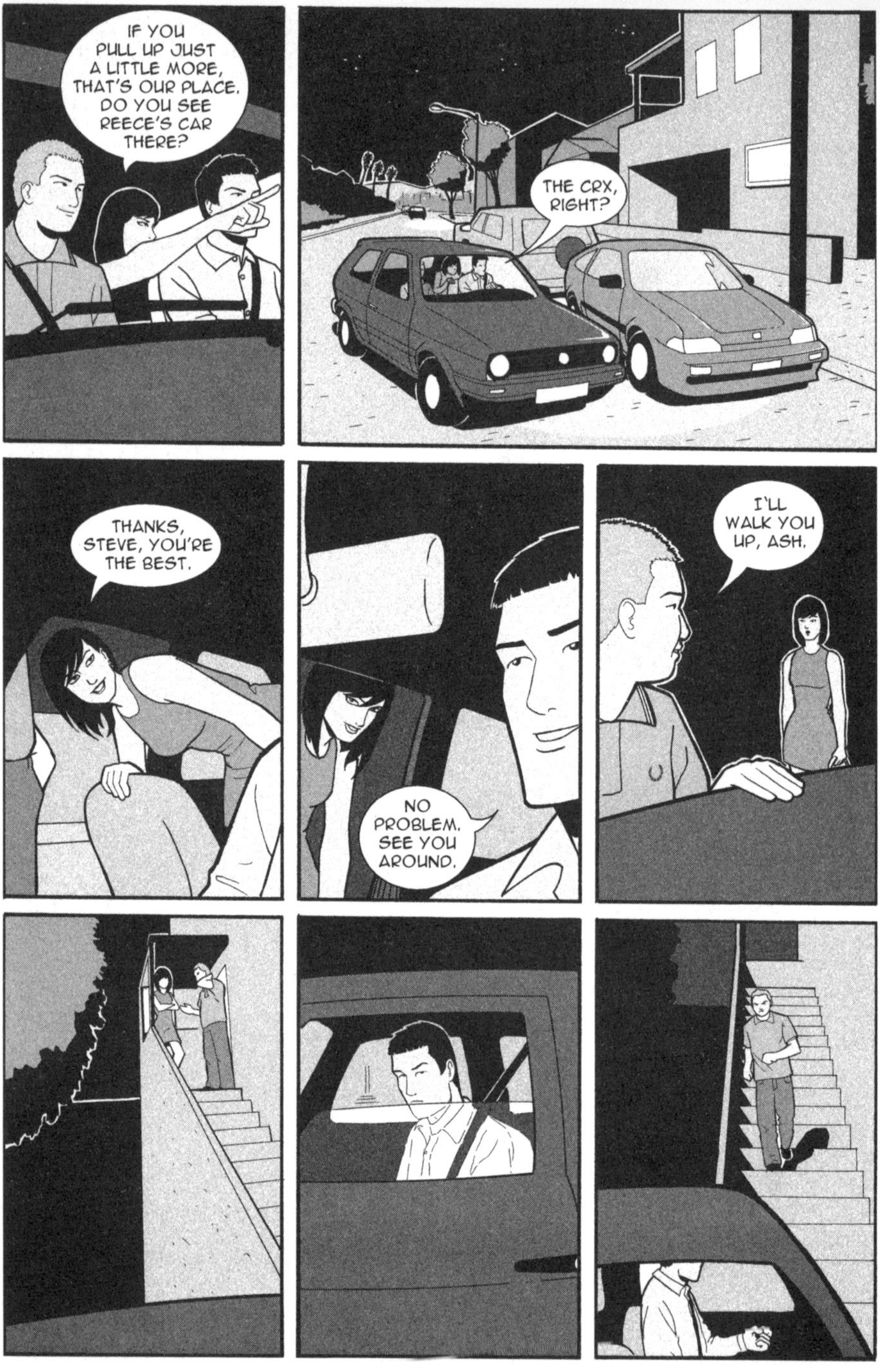
IF YOU PULL UP JUST A LITTLE MORE, THAT'S OUR PLACE. DO YOU SEE REECE'S CAR THERE?
THE CRX, RIGHT?
THANKS, STEVE, YOU'RE THE BEST.
NO PROBLEM. SEE YOU AROUND.
I'LL WALK YOU UP, ASH.

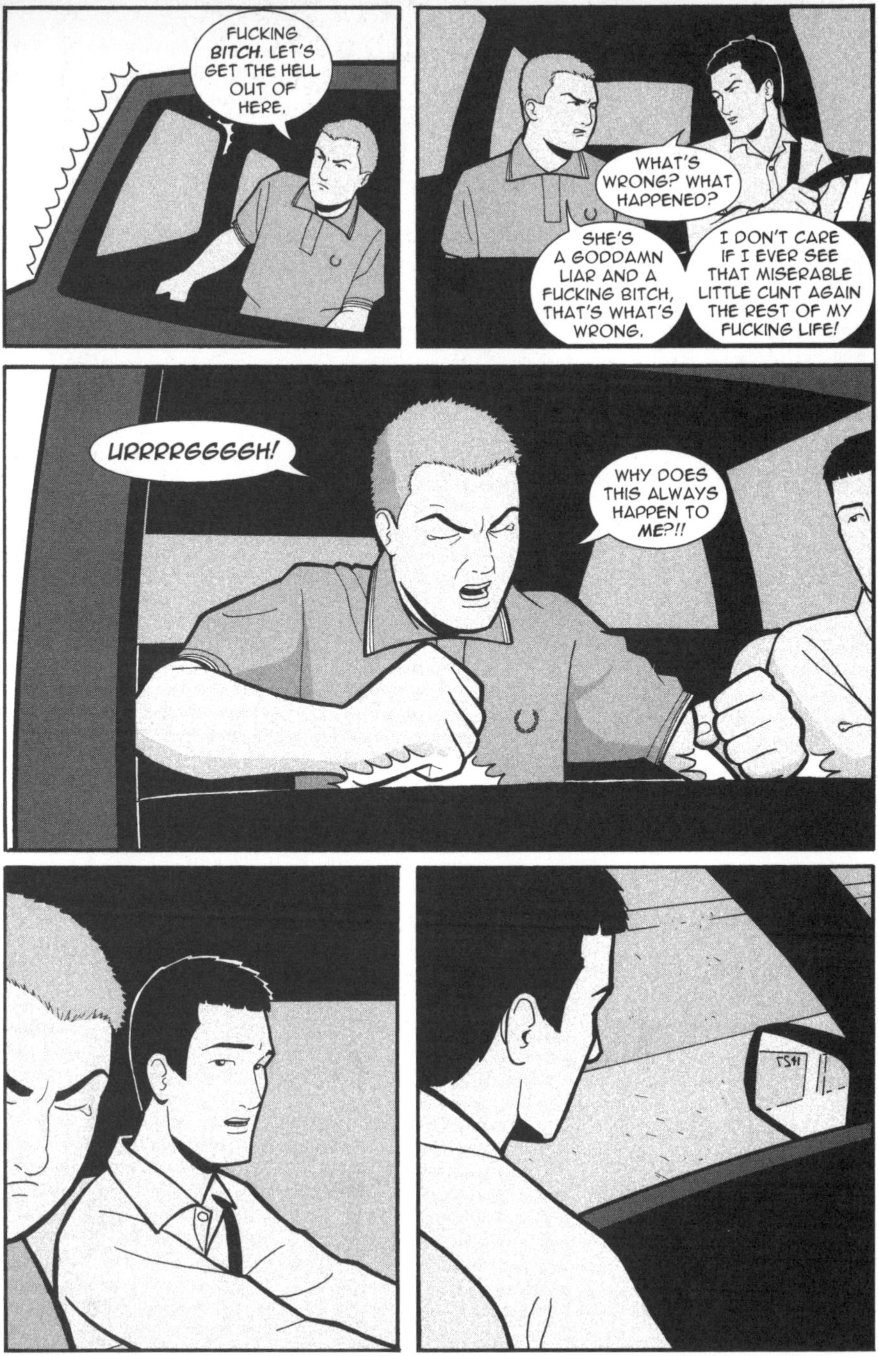
FUCKING BITCH. LET'S GET THE HELL OUT OF HERE.
WHAT'S WRONG? WHAT HAPPENED?
SHE'S A GODDAMN LIAR AND A FUCKING BITCH, THAT'S WHAT'S WRONG.
I DON'T CARE IF I EVER SEE THAT MISERABLE LITTLE CUNT AGAIN THE REST OF MY FUCKING LIFE!
URRRRGGGGH!
WHY DOES THIS ALWAYS HAPPEN TO ME?!!

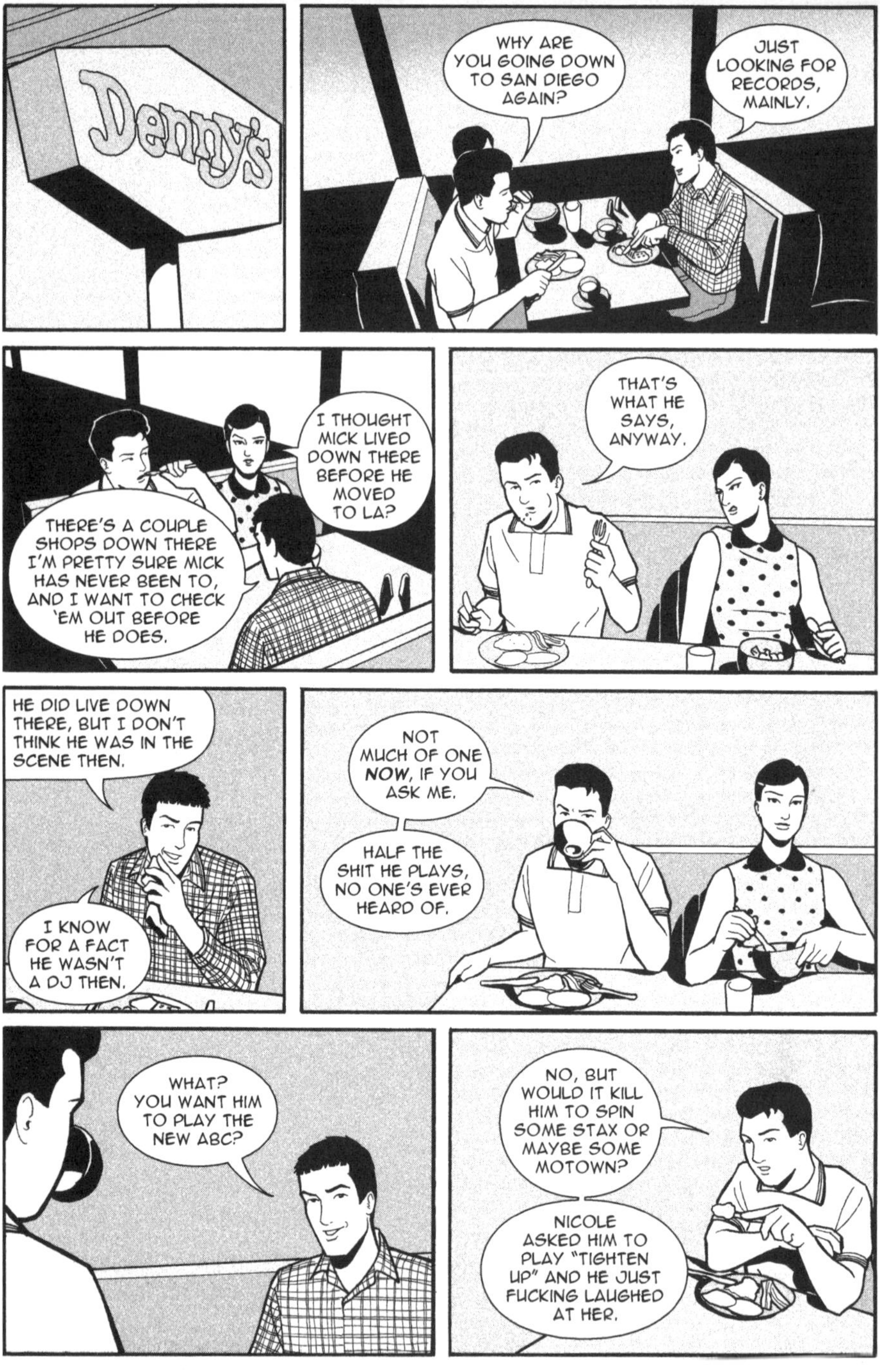
Denny's
WHY ARE YOU GOING DOWN TO SAN DIEGO AGAIN?
JUST LOOKING FOR RECORDS, MAINLY.
I THOUGHT MICK LIVED DOWN THERE BEFORE HE MOVED TO LA?
THERE'S A COUPLE SHOPS DOWN THERE I'M PRETTY SURE MICK HAS NEVER BEEN TO, AND I WANT TO CHECK 'EM OUT BEFORE HE DOES.
THAT'S WHAT HE SAYS, ANYWAY.
HE DID LIVE DOWN THERE, BUT I DON'T THINK HE WAS IN THE SCENE THEN.
I KNOW FOR A FACT HE WASN'T A DJ THEN.
NOT MUCH OF ONE NOW, IF YOU ASK ME.
HALF THE SHIT HE PLAYS, NO ONE'S EVER HEARD OF.
WHAT? YOU WANT HIM TO PLAY THE NEW ABC?
NO, BUT WOULD IT KILL HIM TO SPIN SOME STAX OR MAYBE SOME MOTOWN?
NICOLE ASKED HIM TO PLAY "TIGHTEN UP" AND HE JUST FUCKING LAUGHED AT HER.

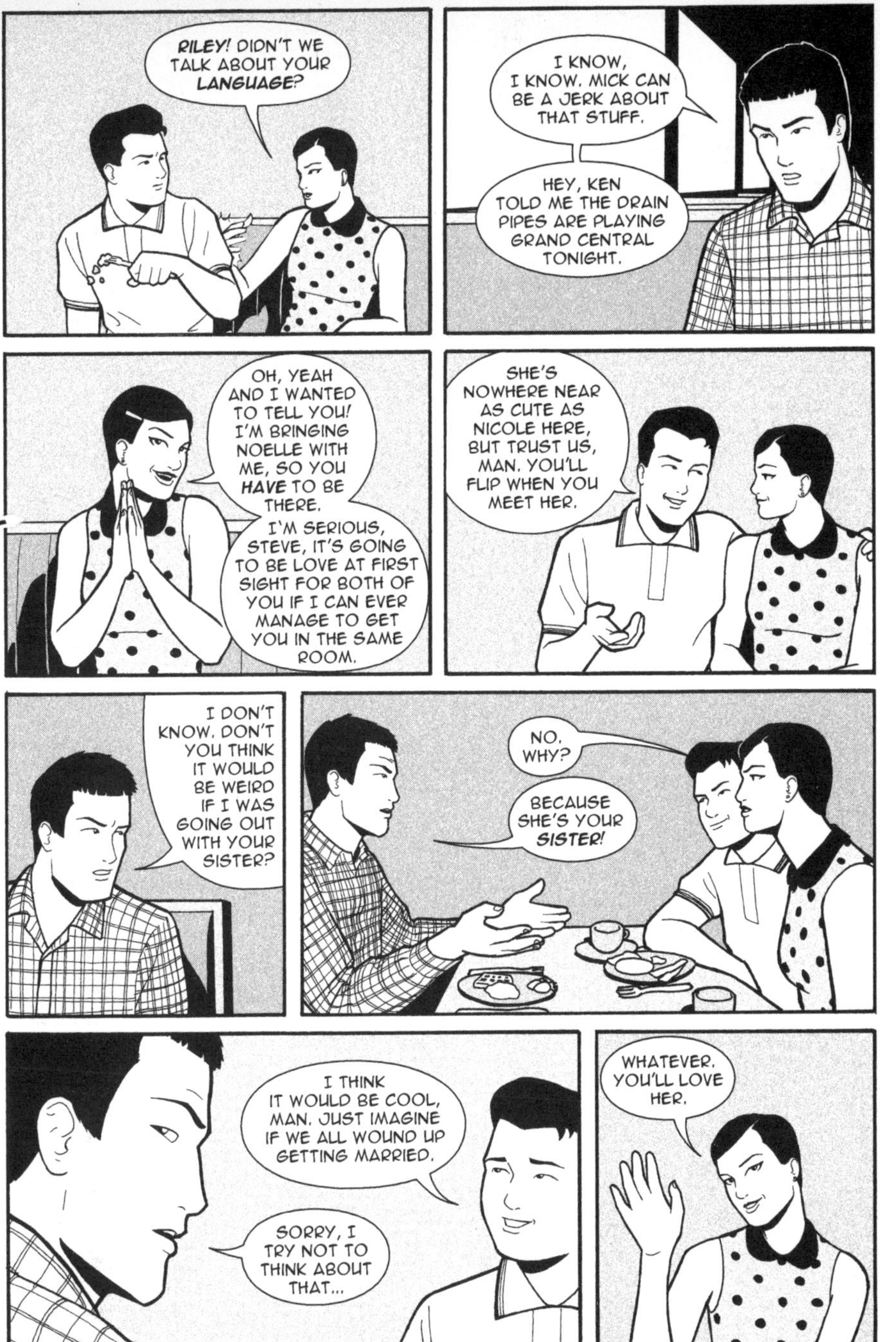
RILEY! DIDN'T WE TALK ABOUT YOUR LANGUAGE?
I KNOW, I KNOW. MICK CAN BE A JERK ABOUT THAT STUFF.
HEY, KEN TOLD ME THE DRAIN PIPES ARE PLAYING GRAND CENTRAL TONIGHT.
OH, YEAH AND I WANTED TO TELL YOU! I'M BRINGING NOELLE WITH ME, SO YOU HAVE TO BE THERE.
I'M SERIOUS, STEVE, IT'S GOING TO BE LOVE AT FIRST SIGHT FOR BOTH OF YOU IF I CAN EVER MANAGE TO GET YOU IN THE SAME ROOM.
SHE'S NOWHERE NEAR AS CUTE AS NICOLE HERE, BUT TRUST US, MAN. YOU'LL FLIP WHEN YOU MEET HER.
I DON'T KNOW. DON'T YOU THINK IT WOULD BE WEIRD IF I WAS GOING OUT WITH YOUR SISTER?
NO. WHY?
BECAUSE SHE'S YOUR SISTER!
I THINK IT WOULD BE COOL, MAN. JUST IMAGINE IF WE ALL WOUND UP GETTING MARRIED.
SORRY, I TRY NOT TO THINK ABOUT THAT...
WHATEVER. YOU'LL LOVE HER.

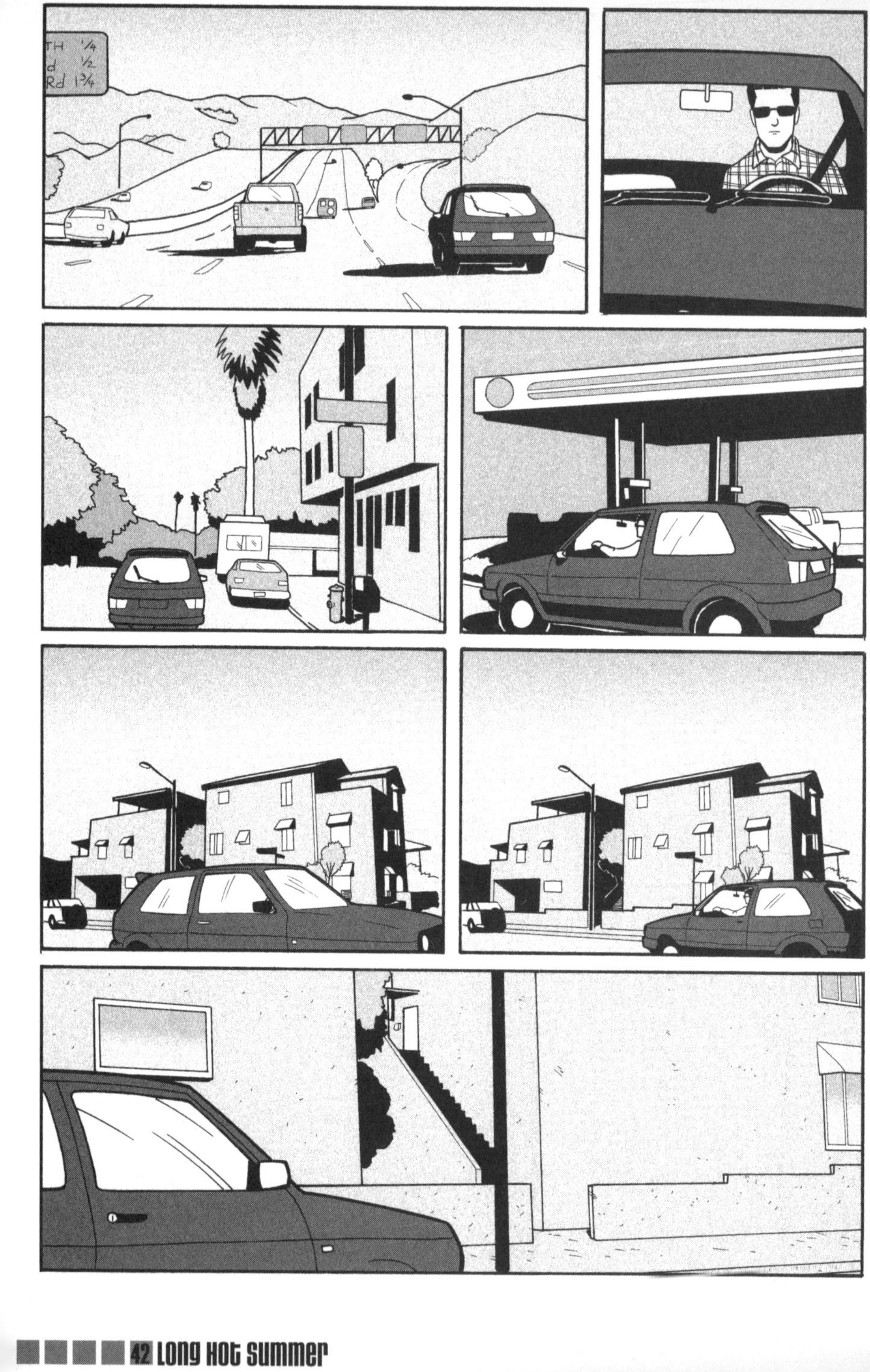
TH 1/4
d 1/2
Rd 1 3/4

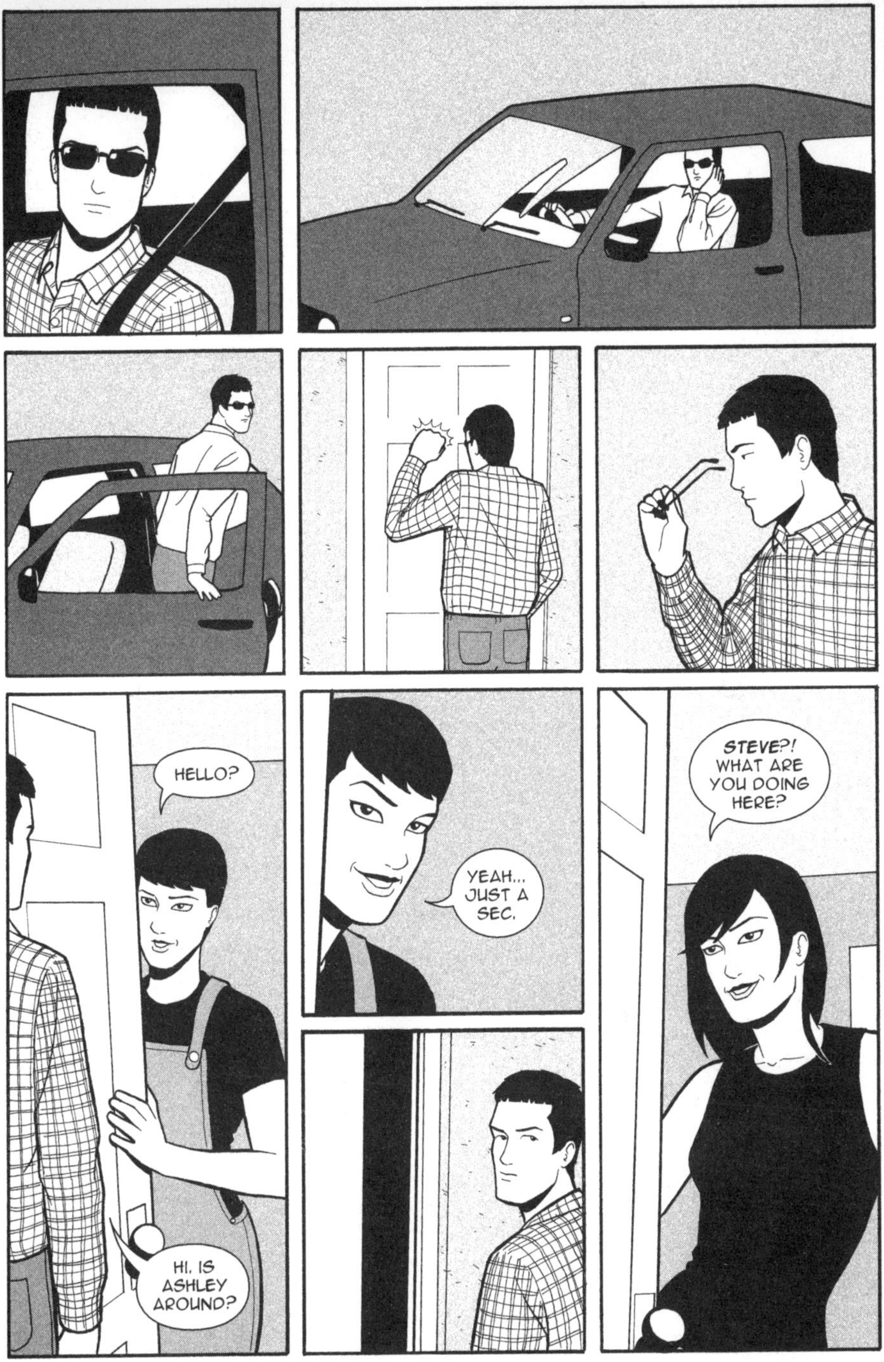
HELLO?
HI. IS ASHLEY AROUND?
YEAH... JUST A SEC.
STEVE?! WHAT ARE YOU DOING HERE?

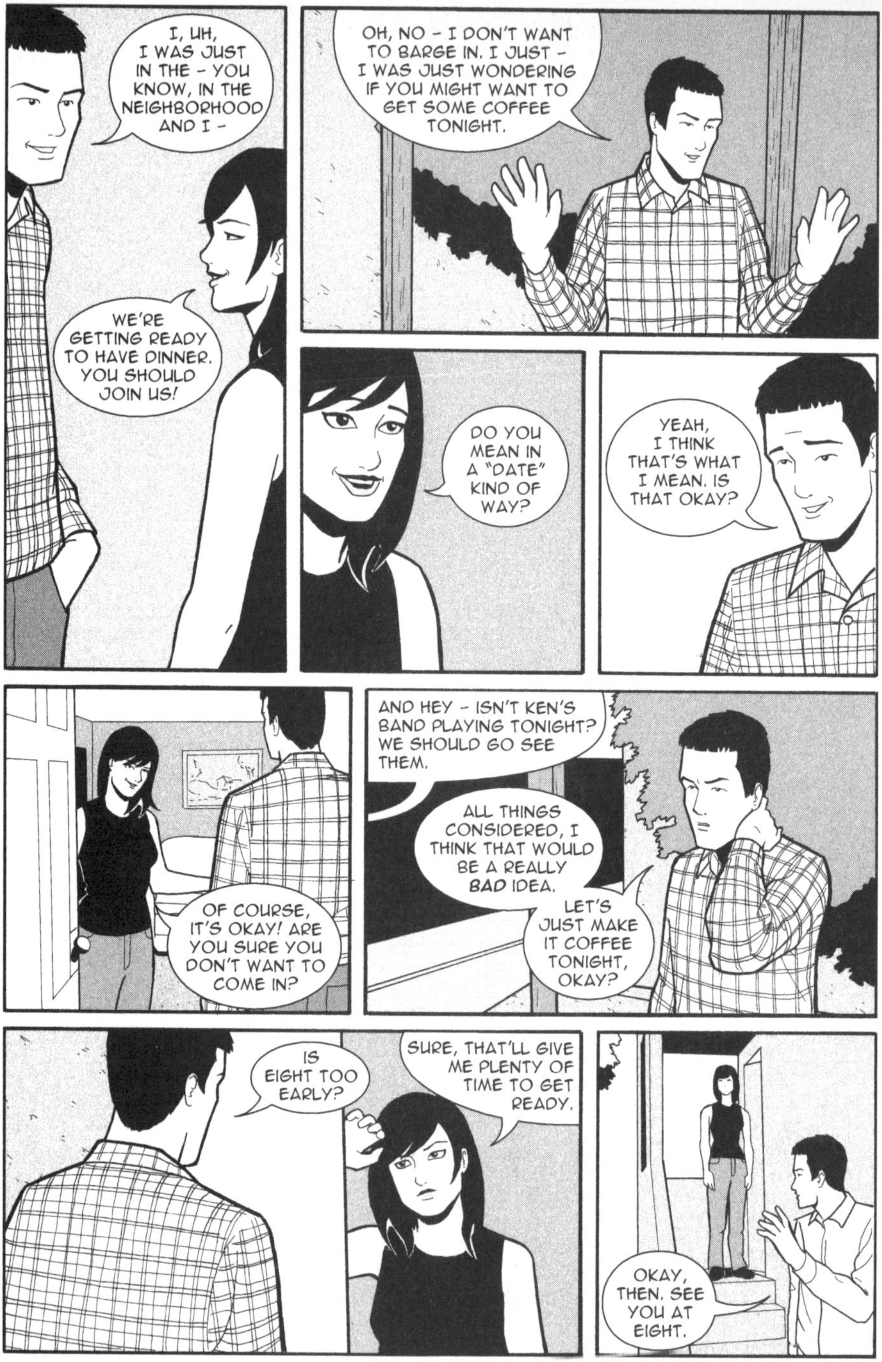
I, UH, I WAS JUST IN THE - YOU KNOW, IN THE NEIGHBORHOOD AND I -
WE'RE GETTING READY TO HAVE DINNER. YOU SHOULD JOIN US!
OH, NO - I DON'T WANT TO BARGE IN. I JUST - I WAS JUST WONDERING IF YOU MIGHT WANT TO GET SOME COFFEE TONIGHT.
DO YOU MEAN IN A "DATE" KIND OF WAY?
YEAH, I THINK THAT'S WHAT I MEAN. IS THAT OKAY?
OF COURSE, IT'S OKAY! ARE YOU SURE YOU DON'T WANT TO COME IN?
AND HEY - ISN'T KEN'S BAND PLAYING TONIGHT? WE SHOULD GO SEE THEM.
ALL THINGS CONSIDERED, I THINK THAT WOULD BE A REALLY BAD IDEA.
LET'S JUST MAKE IT COFFEE TONIGHT, OKAY?
IS EIGHT TOO EARLY?
SURE, THAT'LL GIVE ME PLENTY OF TIME TO GET READY.
OKAY, THEN. SEE YOU AT EIGHT.

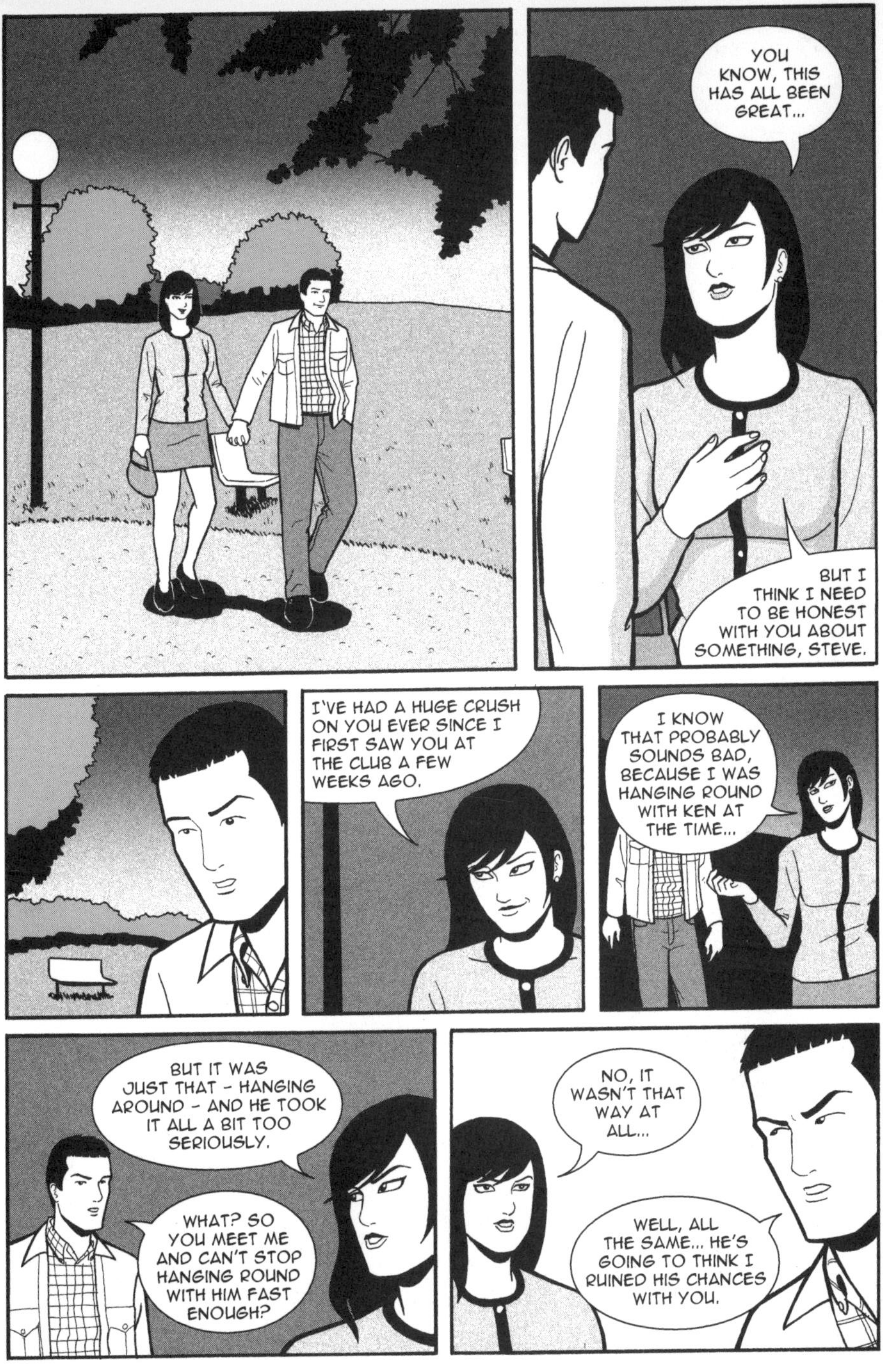
YOU KNOW, THIS HAS ALL BEEN GREAT...
BUT I THINK I NEED TO BE HONEST WITH YOU ABOUT SOMETHING, STEVE.
I'VE HAD A HUGE CRUSH ON YOU EVER SINCE I FIRST SAW YOU AT THE CLUB A FEW WEEKS AGO.
I KNOW THAT PROBABLY SOUNDS BAD, BECAUSE I WAS HANGING ROUND WITH KEN AT THE TIME...
BUT IT WAS JUST THAT - HANGING AROUND - AND HE TOOK IT ALL A BIT TOO SERIOUSLY.
WHAT? SO YOU MEET ME AND CAN'T STOP HANGING ROUND WITH HIM FAST ENOUGH?
NO, IT WASN'T THAT WAY AT ALL...
WELL, ALL THE SAME... HE'S GOING TO THINK I RUINED HIS CHANCES WITH YOU.

LET HIM THINK WHAT HE WANTS.

IT'S NOT *MY* FAULT HE TOOK THINGS THE WRONG WAY, AND IT'S *DEFINITELY* NOT YOUR FAULT.

THAT DOESN'T MAKE ME FEEL MUCH BETTER.

AND KEN'S GOING TO BE MISERABLE.

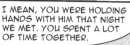

I MEAN, YOU WERE HOLDING HANDS WITH HIM THAT NIGHT WE MET. YOU SPENT A LOT OF TIME TOGETHER.

HOW COULD YOU EXPECT HIM TO THINK YOU WERE JUST FRIENDS?

IT'S NOT LIKE I DUMPED HIM FOR YOU, IF THAT'S WHAT YOU THINK. I DIDN'T EVEN KNOW IF YOU LIKED ME.

BUT I KNEW I DIDN'T WANT TO STAY WITH KEN IF THERE WAS A CHANCE YOU DID.

RIGHT. WELL, IT'S AN AWKWARD SITUATION.

KEN'S GOING THROUGH HELL RIGHT NOW, THANKS TO YOU.

THAT DIDN'T STOP YOU FROM ASKING ME OUT, THOUGH, DID IT?

NO... I GUESS IT DIDN'T.

SHIT.

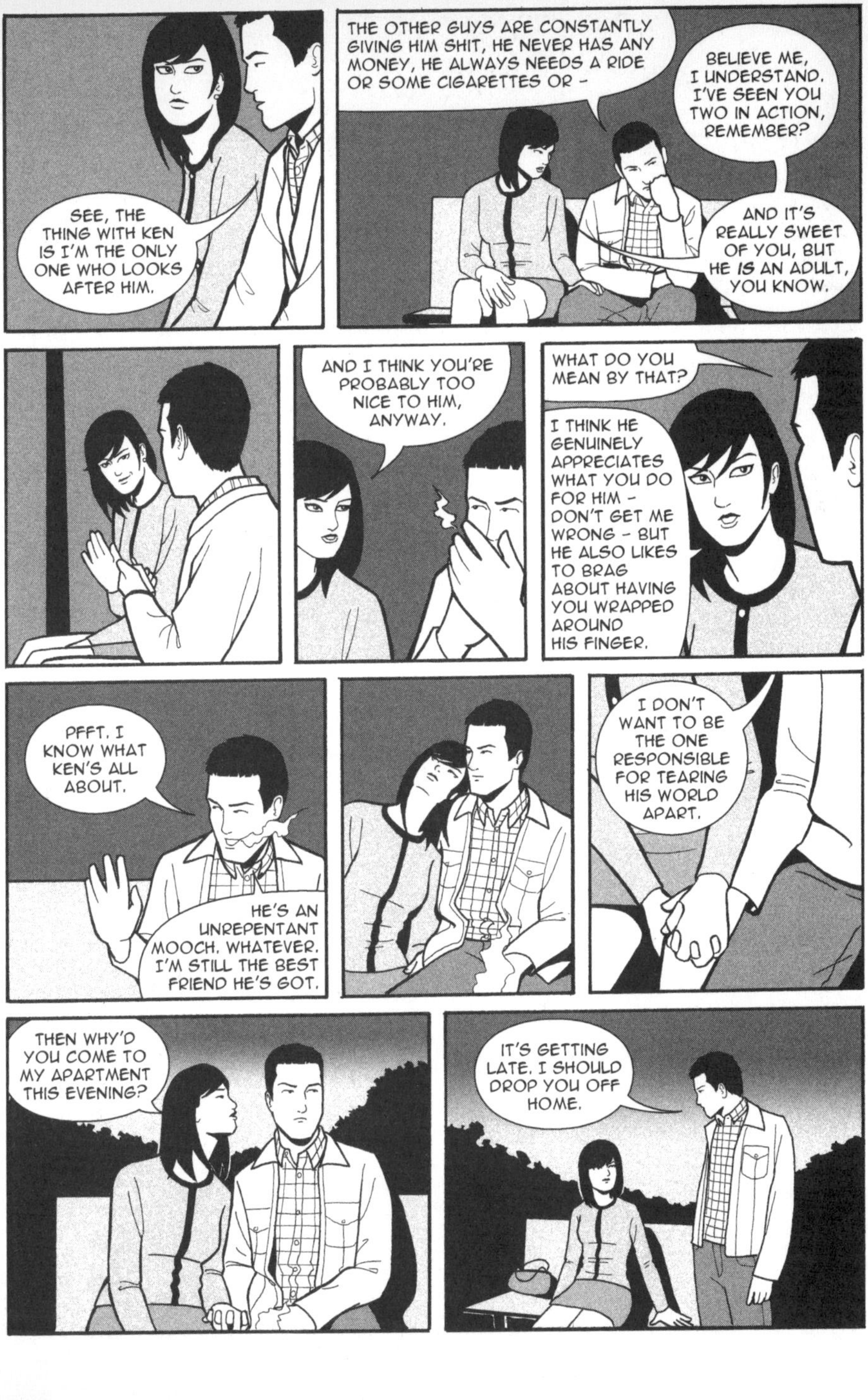
SEE, THE THING WITH KEN IS I'M THE ONLY ONE WHO LOOKS AFTER HIM.
THE OTHER GUYS ARE CONSTANTLY GIVING HIM SHIT, HE NEVER HAS ANY MONEY, HE ALWAYS NEEDS A RIDE OR SOME CIGARETTES OR –
BELIEVE ME, I UNDERSTAND. I'VE SEEN YOU TWO IN ACTION, REMEMBER?
AND IT'S REALLY SWEET OF YOU, BUT HE *IS* AN ADULT, YOU KNOW.
AND I THINK YOU'RE PROBABLY TOO NICE TO HIM, ANYWAY.
WHAT DO YOU MEAN BY THAT?
I THINK HE GENUINELY APPRECIATES WHAT YOU DO FOR HIM – DON'T GET ME WRONG – BUT HE ALSO LIKES TO BRAG ABOUT HAVING YOU WRAPPED AROUND HIS FINGER.
PFFT. I KNOW WHAT KEN'S ALL ABOUT.
HE'S AN UNREPENTANT MOOCH. WHATEVER. I'M STILL THE BEST FRIEND HE'S GOT.
I DON'T WANT TO BE THE ONE RESPONSIBLE FOR TEARING HIS WORLD APART.
THEN WHY'D YOU COME TO MY APARTMENT THIS EVENING?
IT'S GETTING LATE. I SHOULD DROP YOU OFF HOME.

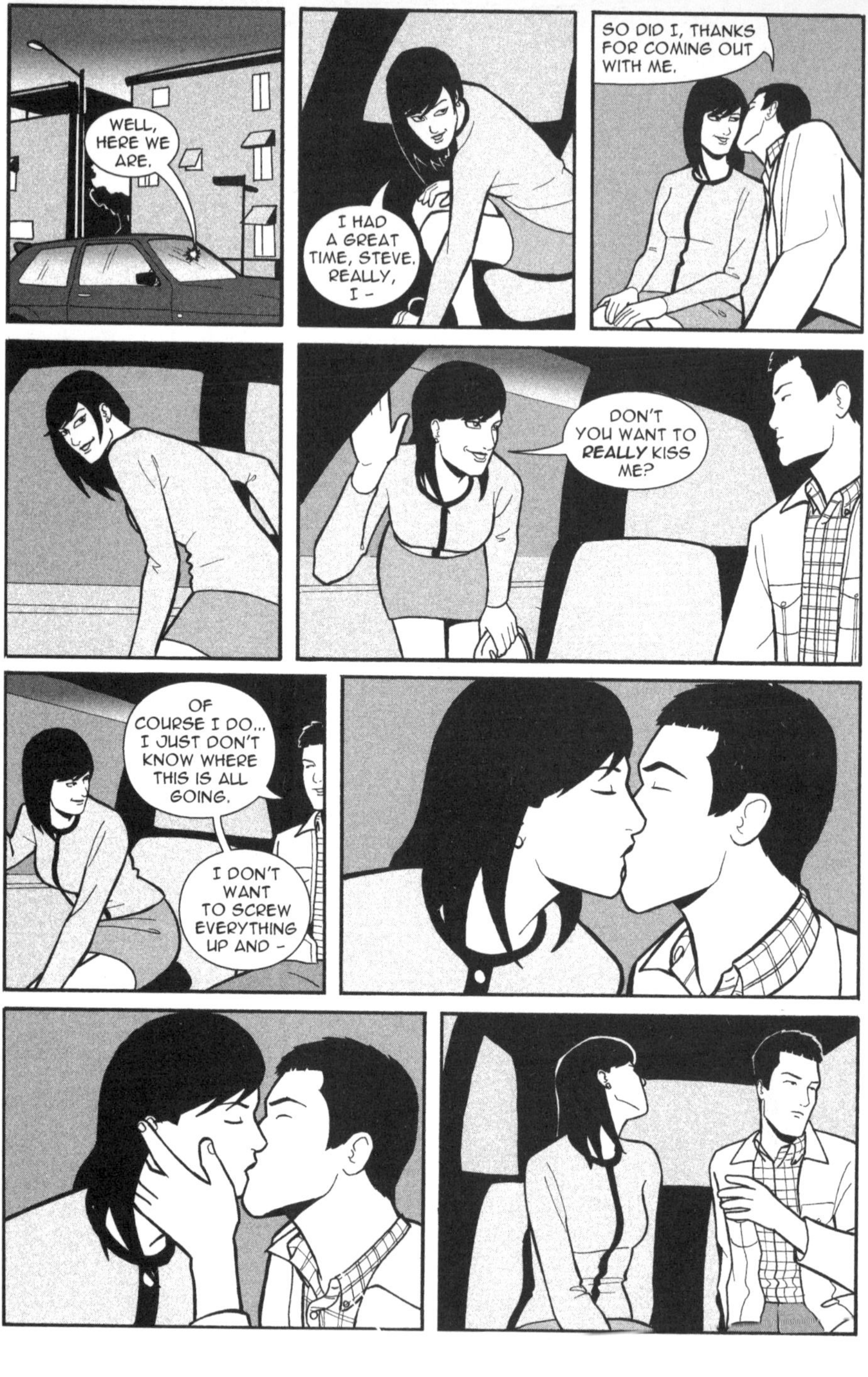
WELL, HERE WE ARE.
I HAD A GREAT TIME, STEVE. REALLY, I -
SO DID I, THANKS FOR COMING OUT WITH ME.
DON'T YOU WANT TO **REALLY** KISS ME?
OF COURSE I DO... I JUST DON'T KNOW WHERE THIS IS ALL GOING.
I DON'T WANT TO SCREW EVERYTHING UP AND -

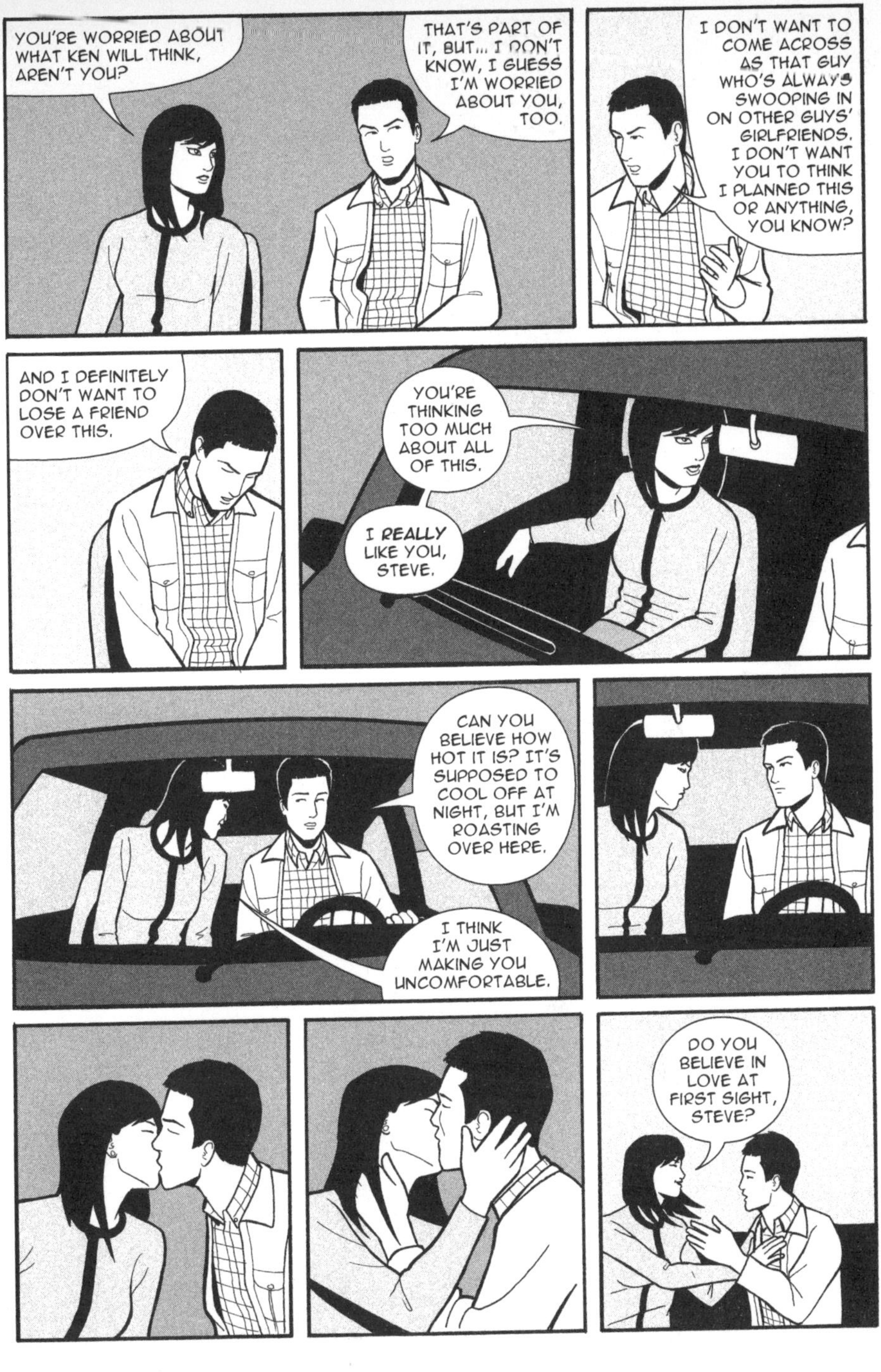
YOU'RE WORRIED ABOUT WHAT KEN WILL THINK, AREN'T YOU?
THAT'S PART OF IT, BUT... I DON'T KNOW, I GUESS I'M WORRIED ABOUT YOU, TOO.
I DON'T WANT TO COME ACROSS AS THAT GUY WHO'S ALWAYS SWOOPING IN ON OTHER GUYS' GIRLFRIENDS. I DON'T WANT YOU TO THINK I PLANNED THIS OR ANYTHING, YOU KNOW?
AND I DEFINITELY DON'T WANT TO LOSE A FRIEND OVER THIS.
YOU'RE THINKING TOO MUCH ABOUT ALL OF THIS.
I REALLY LIKE YOU, STEVE.
CAN YOU BELIEVE HOW HOT IT IS? IT'S SUPPOSED TO COOL OFF AT NIGHT, BUT I'M ROASTING OVER HERE.
I THINK I'M JUST MAKING YOU UNCOMFORTABLE.
DO YOU BELIEVE IN LOVE AT FIRST SIGHT, STEVE?

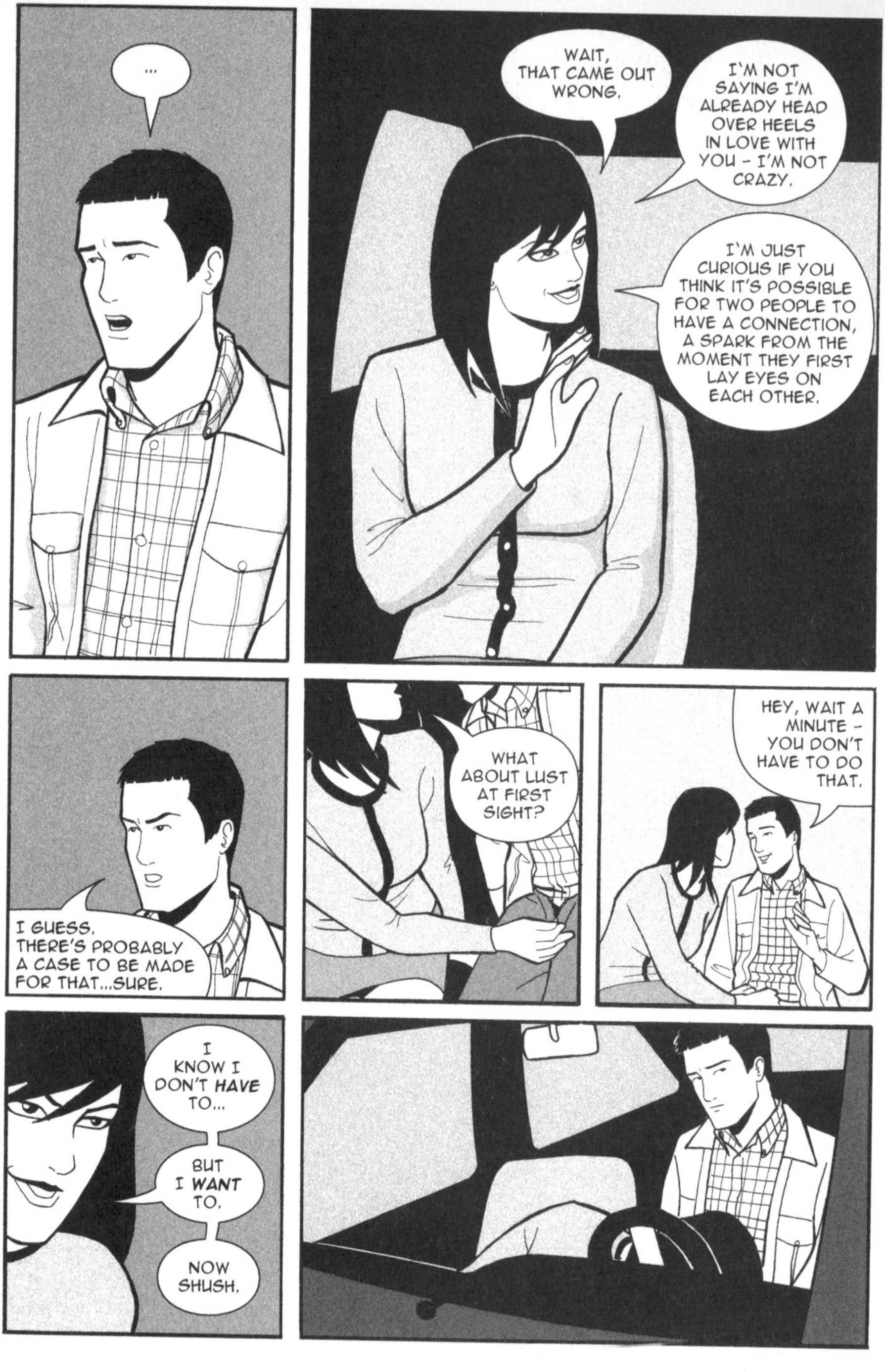
...
WAIT, THAT CAME OUT WRONG.
I'M NOT SAYING I'M ALREADY HEAD OVER HEELS IN LOVE WITH YOU – I'M NOT CRAZY.
I'M JUST CURIOUS IF YOU THINK IT'S POSSIBLE FOR TWO PEOPLE TO HAVE A CONNECTION, A SPARK FROM THE MOMENT THEY FIRST LAY EYES ON EACH OTHER.
I GUESS. THERE'S PROBABLY A CASE TO BE MADE FOR THAT...SURE.
WHAT ABOUT LUST AT FIRST SIGHT?
HEY, WAIT A MINUTE – YOU DON'T HAVE TO DO THAT.
I KNOW I DON'T **HAVE** TO...
BUT I **WANT** TO.
NOW SHUSH.

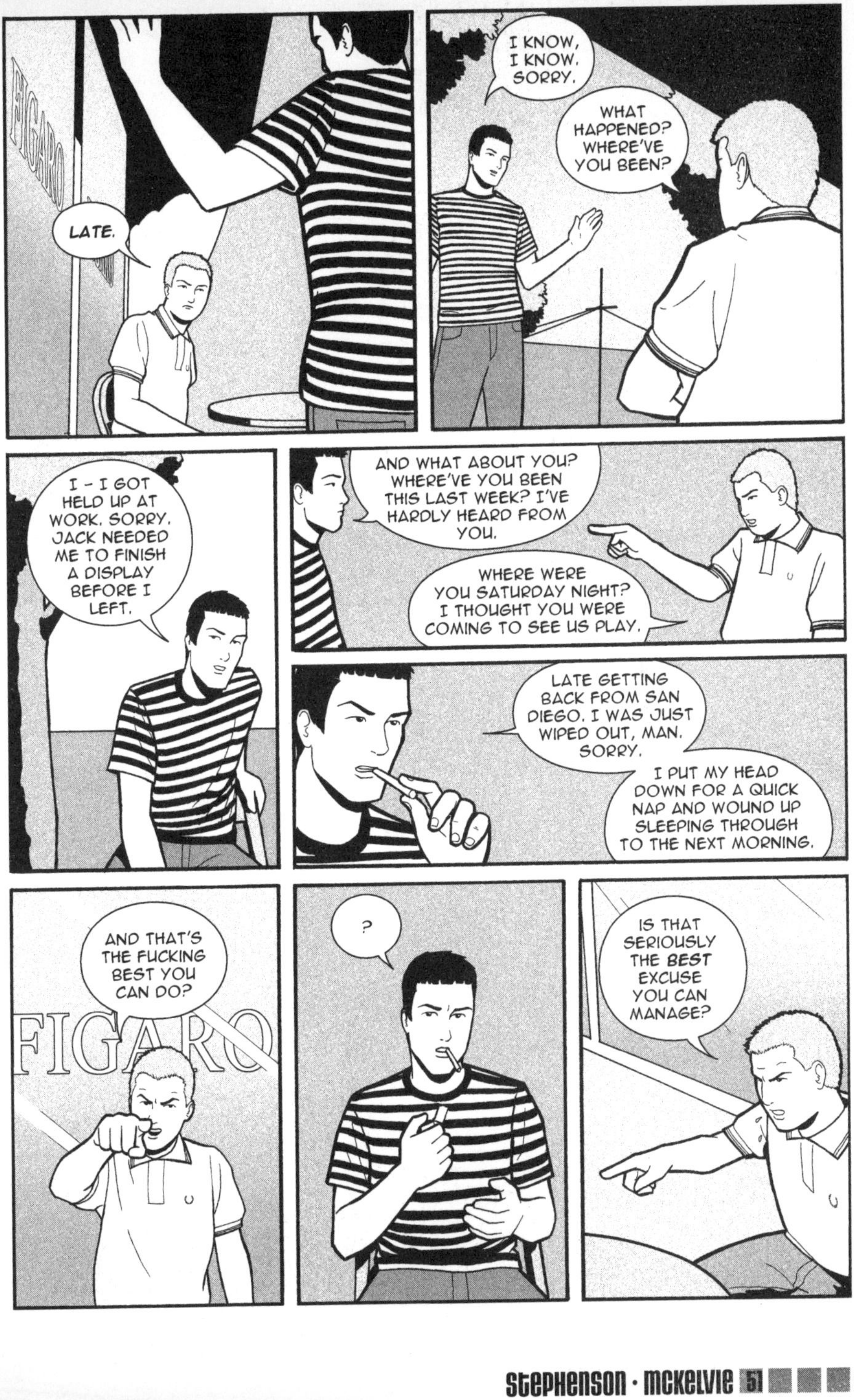
FIGARO
LATE.
I KNOW, I KNOW. SORRY.
WHAT HAPPENED? WHERE'VE YOU BEEN?
I - I GOT HELD UP AT WORK. SORRY. JACK NEEDED ME TO FINISH A DISPLAY BEFORE I LEFT.
AND WHAT ABOUT YOU? WHERE'VE YOU BEEN THIS LAST WEEK? I'VE HARDLY HEARD FROM YOU.
WHERE WERE YOU SATURDAY NIGHT? I THOUGHT YOU WERE COMING TO SEE US PLAY.
LATE GETTING BACK FROM SAN DIEGO. I WAS JUST WIPED OUT, MAN. SORRY.
I PUT MY HEAD DOWN FOR A QUICK NAP AND WOUND UP SLEEPING THROUGH TO THE NEXT MORNING.
AND THAT'S THE FUCKING BEST YOU CAN DO?
FIGARO
?
IS THAT SERIOUSLY THE BEST EXCUSE YOU CAN MANAGE?

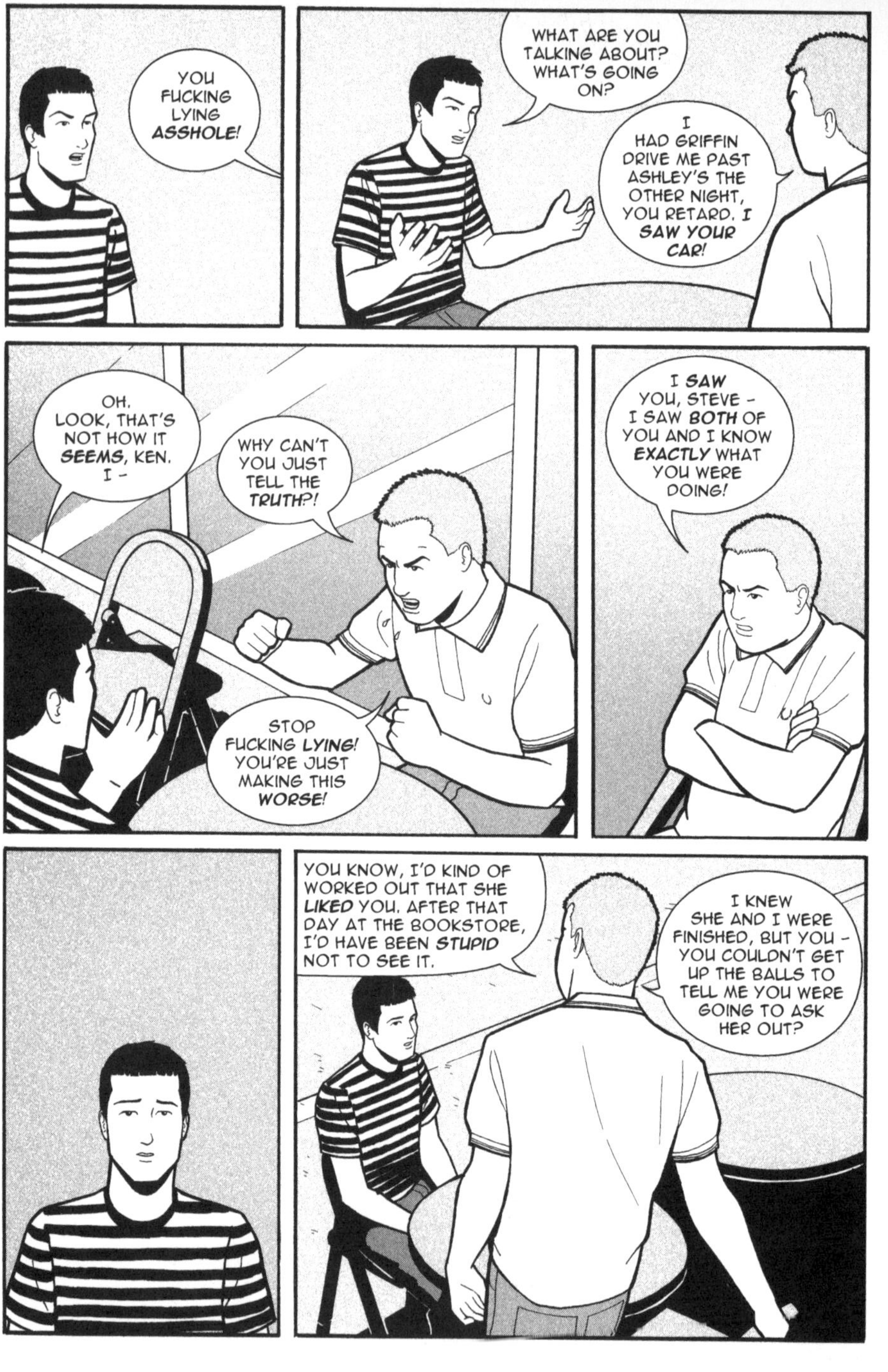
YOU FUCKING LYING ASSHOLE!
WHAT ARE YOU TALKING ABOUT? WHAT'S GOING ON?
I HAD GRIFFIN DRIVE ME PAST ASHLEY'S THE OTHER NIGHT, YOU RETARD. I SAW YOUR CAR!
OH. LOOK, THAT'S NOT HOW IT SEEMS, KEN. I -
WHY CAN'T YOU JUST TELL THE TRUTH?!
STOP FUCKING LYING! YOU'RE JUST MAKING THIS WORSE!
I SAW YOU, STEVE - I SAW BOTH OF YOU AND I KNOW EXACTLY WHAT YOU WERE DOING!
YOU KNOW, I'D KIND OF WORKED OUT THAT SHE LIKED YOU. AFTER THAT DAY AT THE BOOKSTORE, I'D HAVE BEEN STUPID NOT TO SEE IT.
I KNEW SHE AND I WERE FINISHED, BUT YOU - YOU COULDN'T GET UP THE BALLS TO TELL ME YOU WERE GOING TO ASK HER OUT?

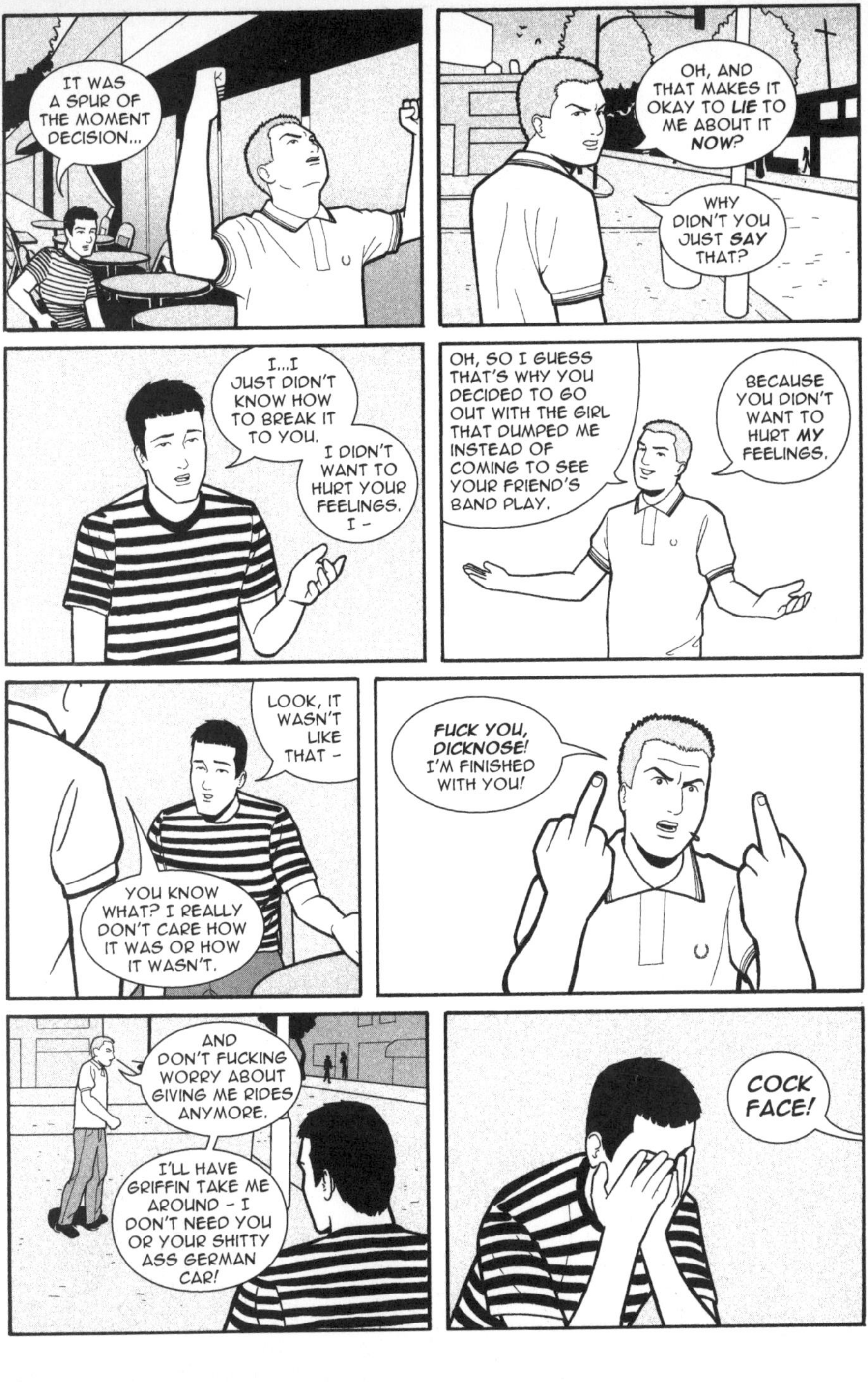
IT WAS A SPUR OF THE MOMENT DECISION...
OH, AND THAT MAKES IT OKAY TO **LIE** TO ME ABOUT IT **NOW?**
WHY DIDN'T YOU JUST **SAY** THAT?
I...I JUST DIDN'T KNOW HOW TO BREAK IT TO YOU.
I DIDN'T WANT TO HURT YOUR FEELINGS. I -
OH, SO I GUESS THAT'S WHY YOU DECIDED TO GO OUT WITH THE GIRL THAT DUMPED ME INSTEAD OF COMING TO SEE YOUR FRIEND'S BAND PLAY.
BECAUSE YOU DIDN'T WANT TO HURT **MY** FEELINGS.
LOOK, IT WASN'T LIKE THAT -
YOU KNOW WHAT? I REALLY DON'T CARE HOW IT WAS OR HOW IT WASN'T.
FUCK YOU, DICKNOSE! I'M FINISHED WITH YOU!
AND DON'T FUCKING WORRY ABOUT GIVING ME RIDES ANYMORE.
I'LL HAVE GRIFFIN TAKE ME AROUND - I DON'T NEED YOU OR YOUR SHITTY ASS GERMAN CAR!
COCK FACE!

I TOLD YOU TO KNOCK THAT OFF – SUZETTE AND REECE ARE GOING TO BE HOME ANY SECOND NOW!

DIDN'T YOU SAY THE SAME THING HALF AN HOUR AGO?

THEY'RE LATE, BUT THEY'LL BE HERE, SO STOP IT.

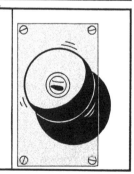

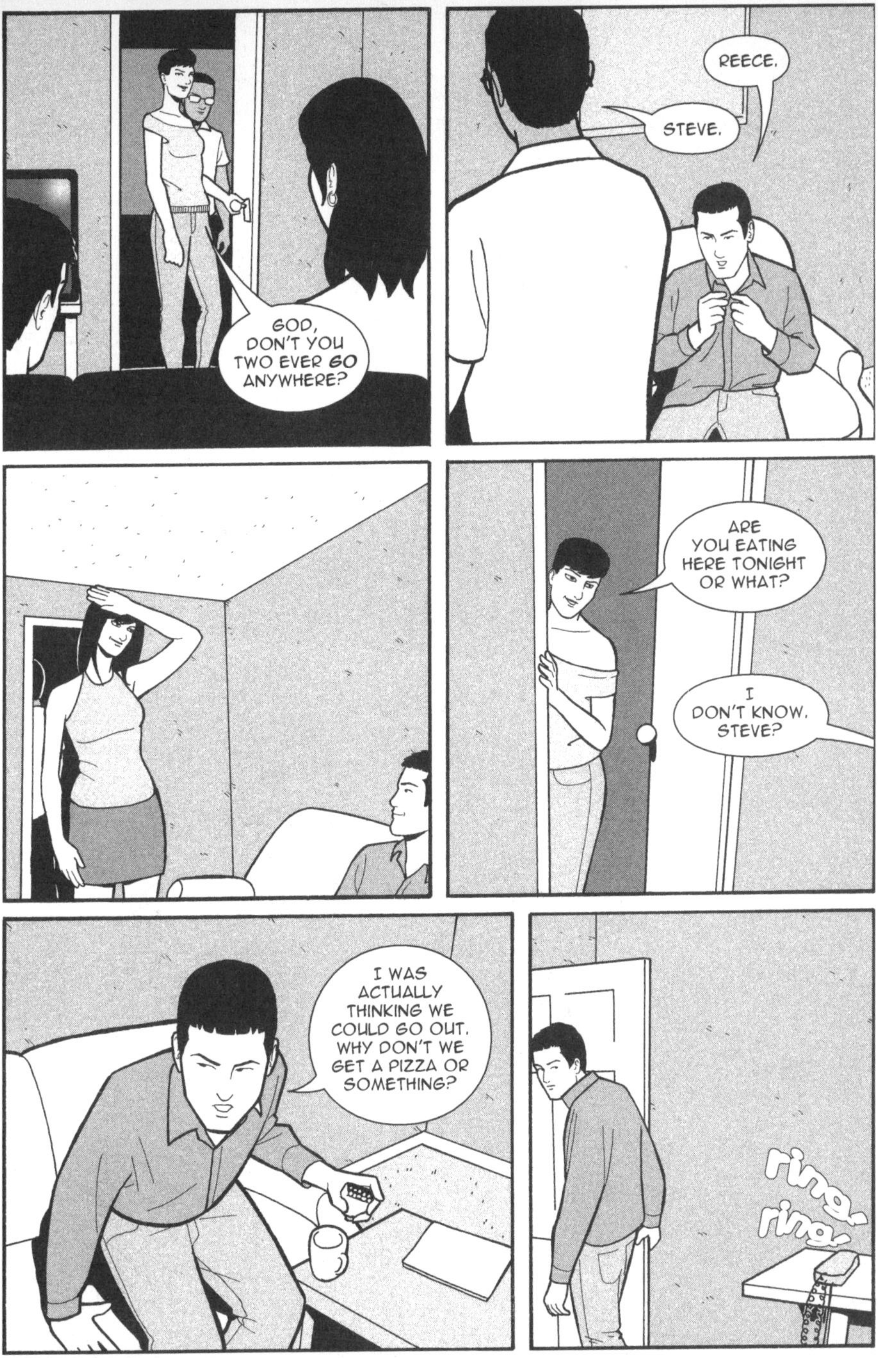
GOD, DON'T YOU TWO EVER GO ANYWHERE?
REECE.
STEVE.
ARE YOU EATING HERE TONIGHT OR WHAT?
I DON'T KNOW. STEVE?
I WAS ACTUALLY THINKING WE COULD GO OUT. WHY DON'T WE GET A PIZZA OR SOMETHING?
ring!
ring!

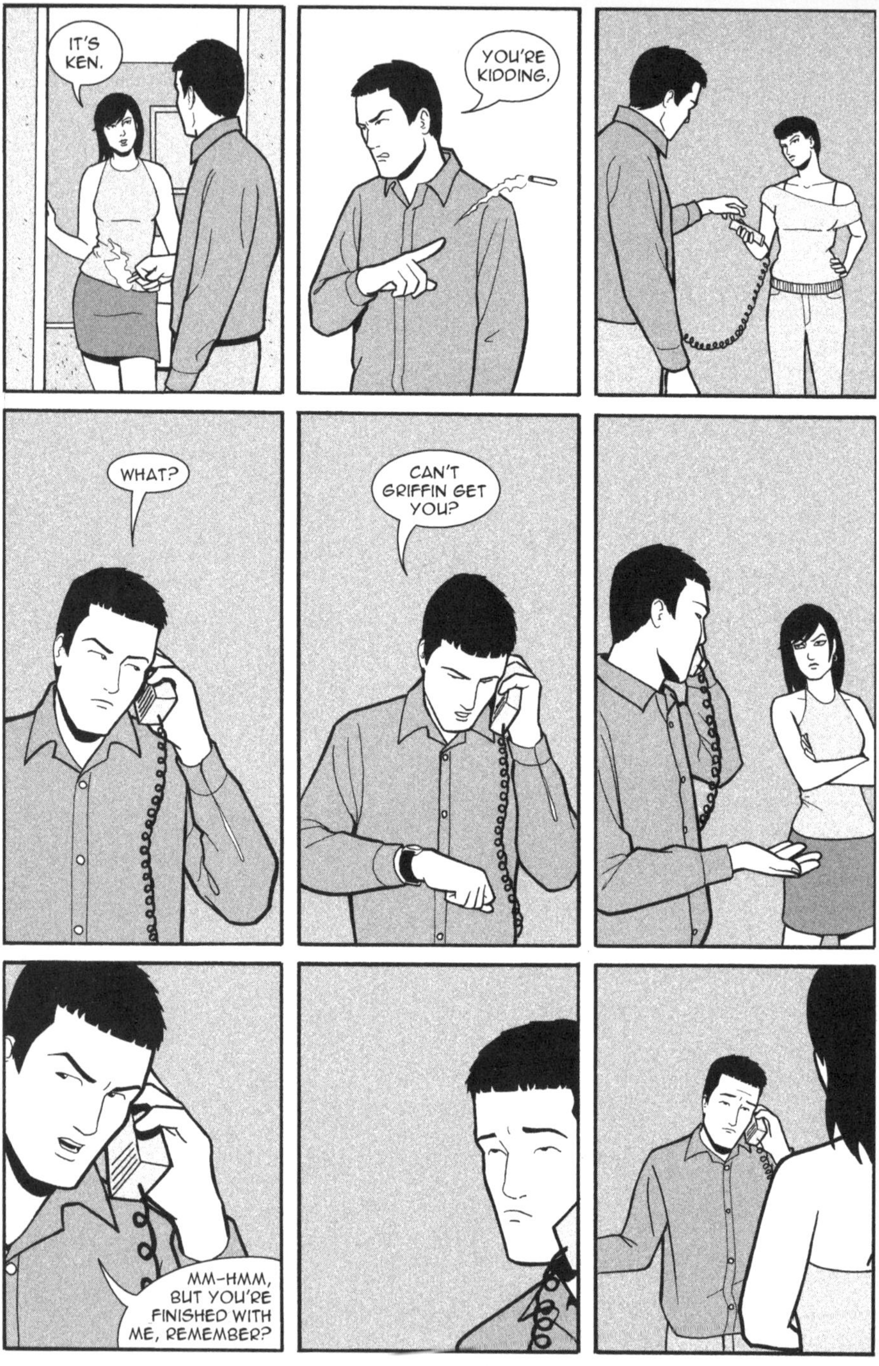
IT'S KEN.
YOU'RE KIDDING.
WHAT?
CAN'T GRIFFIN GET YOU?
MM-HMM, BUT YOU'RE FINISHED WITH ME, REMEMBER?

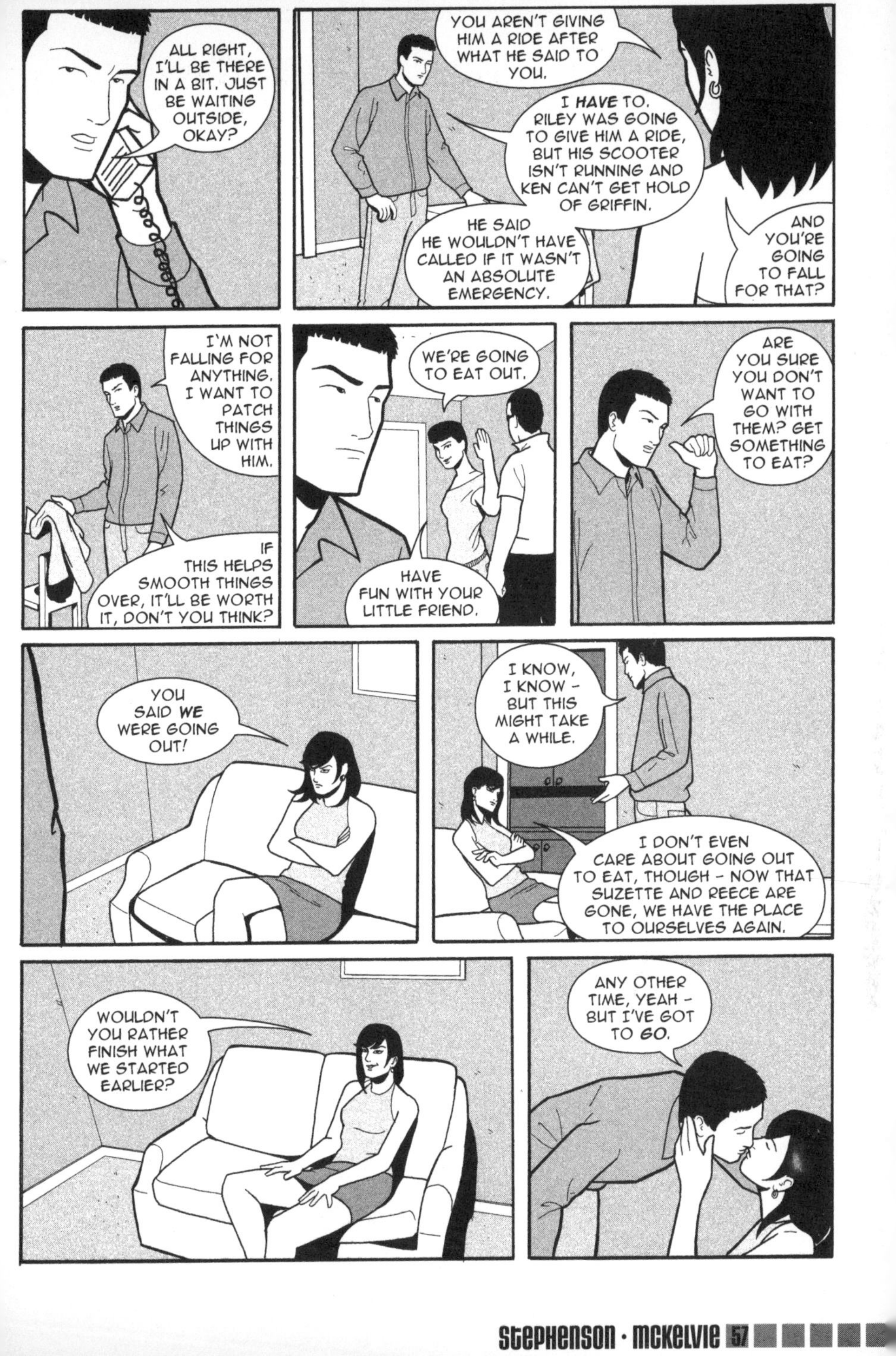
ALL RIGHT, I'LL BE THERE IN A BIT. JUST BE WAITING OUTSIDE, OKAY?
YOU AREN'T GIVING HIM A RIDE AFTER WHAT HE SAID TO YOU.
I HAVE TO. RILEY WAS GOING TO GIVE HIM A RIDE, BUT HIS SCOOTER ISN'T RUNNING AND KEN CAN'T GET HOLD OF GRIFFIN.
HE SAID HE WOULDN'T HAVE CALLED IF IT WASN'T AN ABSOLUTE EMERGENCY.
AND YOU'RE GOING TO FALL FOR THAT?
I'M NOT FALLING FOR ANYTHING. I WANT TO PATCH THINGS UP WITH HIM.
IF THIS HELPS SMOOTH THINGS OVER, IT'LL BE WORTH IT, DON'T YOU THINK?
WE'RE GOING TO EAT OUT.
HAVE FUN WITH YOUR LITTLE FRIEND.
ARE YOU SURE YOU DON'T WANT TO GO WITH THEM? GET SOMETHING TO EAT?
YOU SAID WE WERE GOING OUT!
I KNOW, I KNOW - BUT THIS MIGHT TAKE A WHILE.
I DON'T EVEN CARE ABOUT GOING OUT TO EAT, THOUGH - NOW THAT SUZETTE AND REECE ARE GONE, WE HAVE THE PLACE TO OURSELVES AGAIN.
WOULDN'T YOU RATHER FINISH WHAT WE STARTED EARLIER?
ANY OTHER TIME, YEAH - BUT I'VE GOT TO GO.

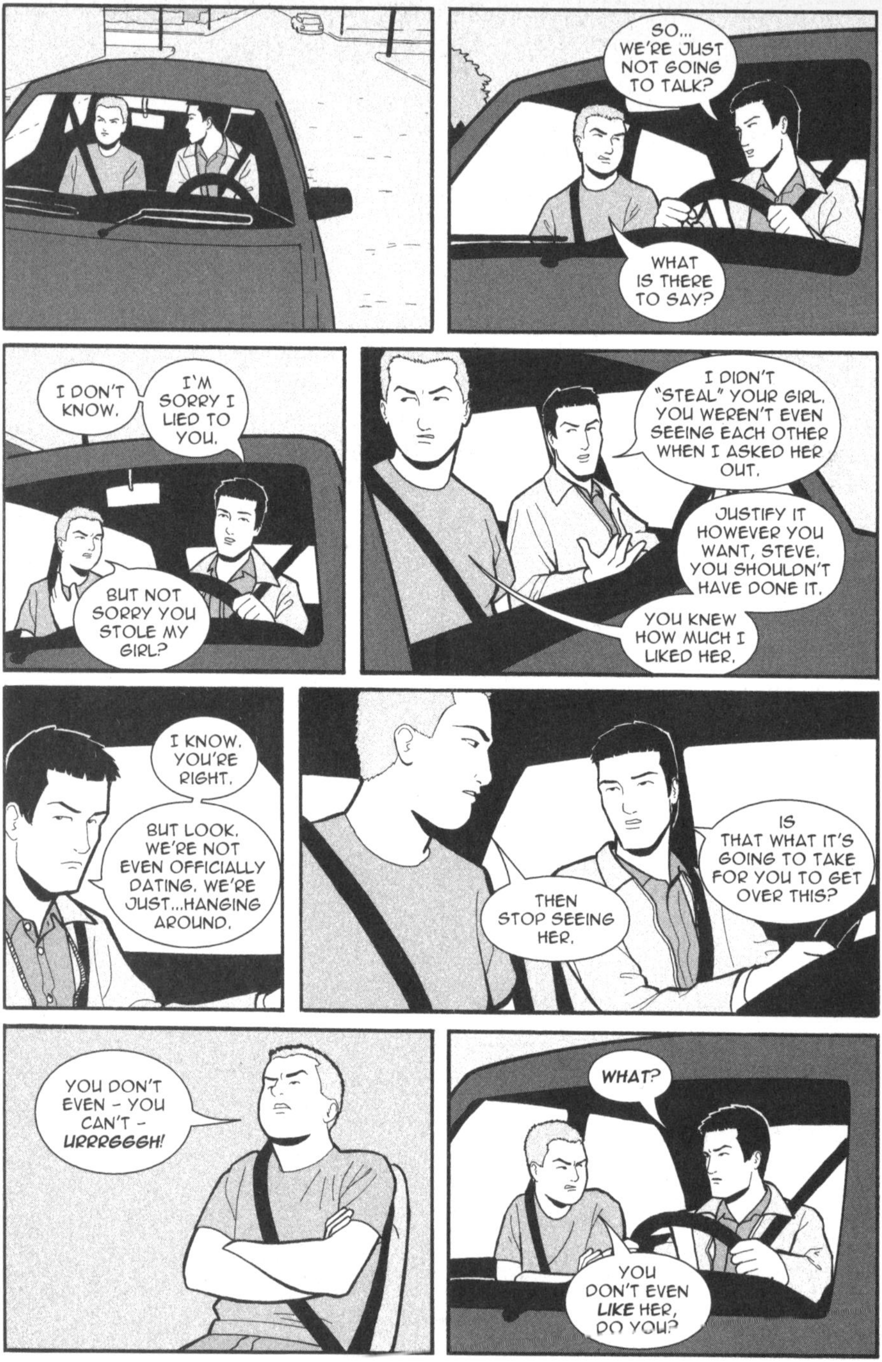
SO... WE'RE JUST NOT GOING TO TALK?
WHAT IS THERE TO SAY?
I DON'T KNOW.
I'M SORRY I LIED TO YOU.
BUT NOT SORRY YOU STOLE MY GIRL?
I DIDN'T "STEAL" YOUR GIRL. YOU WEREN'T EVEN SEEING EACH OTHER WHEN I ASKED HER OUT.
JUSTIFY IT HOWEVER YOU WANT, STEVE. YOU SHOULDN'T HAVE DONE IT.
YOU KNEW HOW MUCH I LIKED HER.
I KNOW. YOU'RE RIGHT.
BUT LOOK. WE'RE NOT EVEN OFFICIALLY DATING. WE'RE JUST...HANGING AROUND.
THEN STOP SEEING HER.
IS THAT WHAT IT'S GOING TO TAKE FOR YOU TO GET OVER THIS?
YOU DON'T EVEN - YOU CAN'T - ***URRRGGGH!***
WHAT?
YOU DON'T EVEN **LIKE** HER, DO YOU?

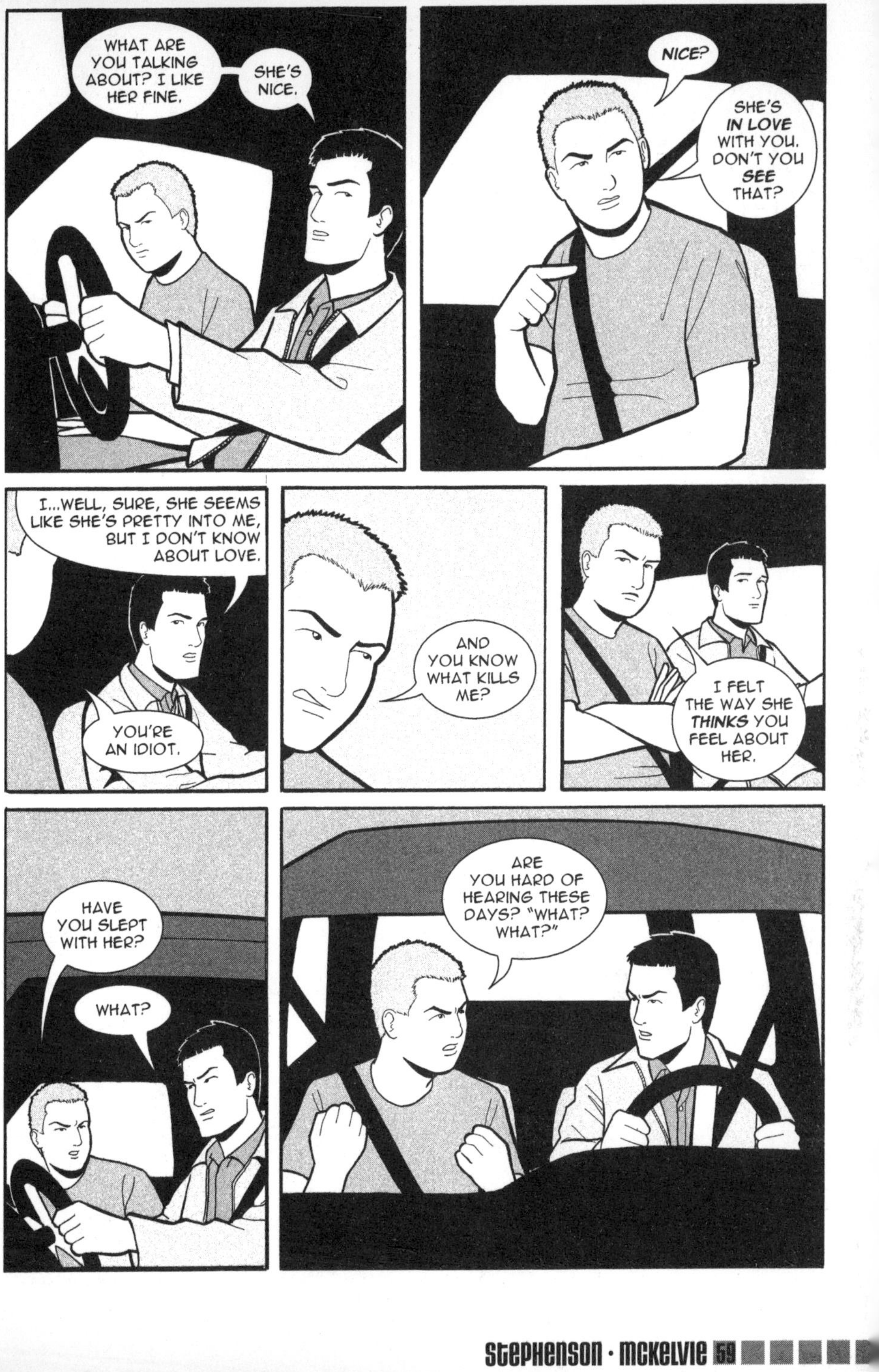

WHAT ARE YOU TALKING ABOUT? I LIKE HER FINE.
SHE'S NICE.
NICE?
SHE'S IN LOVE WITH YOU. DON'T YOU SEE THAT?
I...WELL, SURE, SHE SEEMS LIKE SHE'S PRETTY INTO ME, BUT I DON'T KNOW ABOUT LOVE.
YOU'RE AN IDIOT.
AND YOU KNOW WHAT KILLS ME?
I FELT THE WAY SHE THINKS YOU FEEL ABOUT HER.
HAVE YOU SLEPT WITH HER?
WHAT?
ARE YOU HARD OF HEARING THESE DAYS? "WHAT? WHAT?"

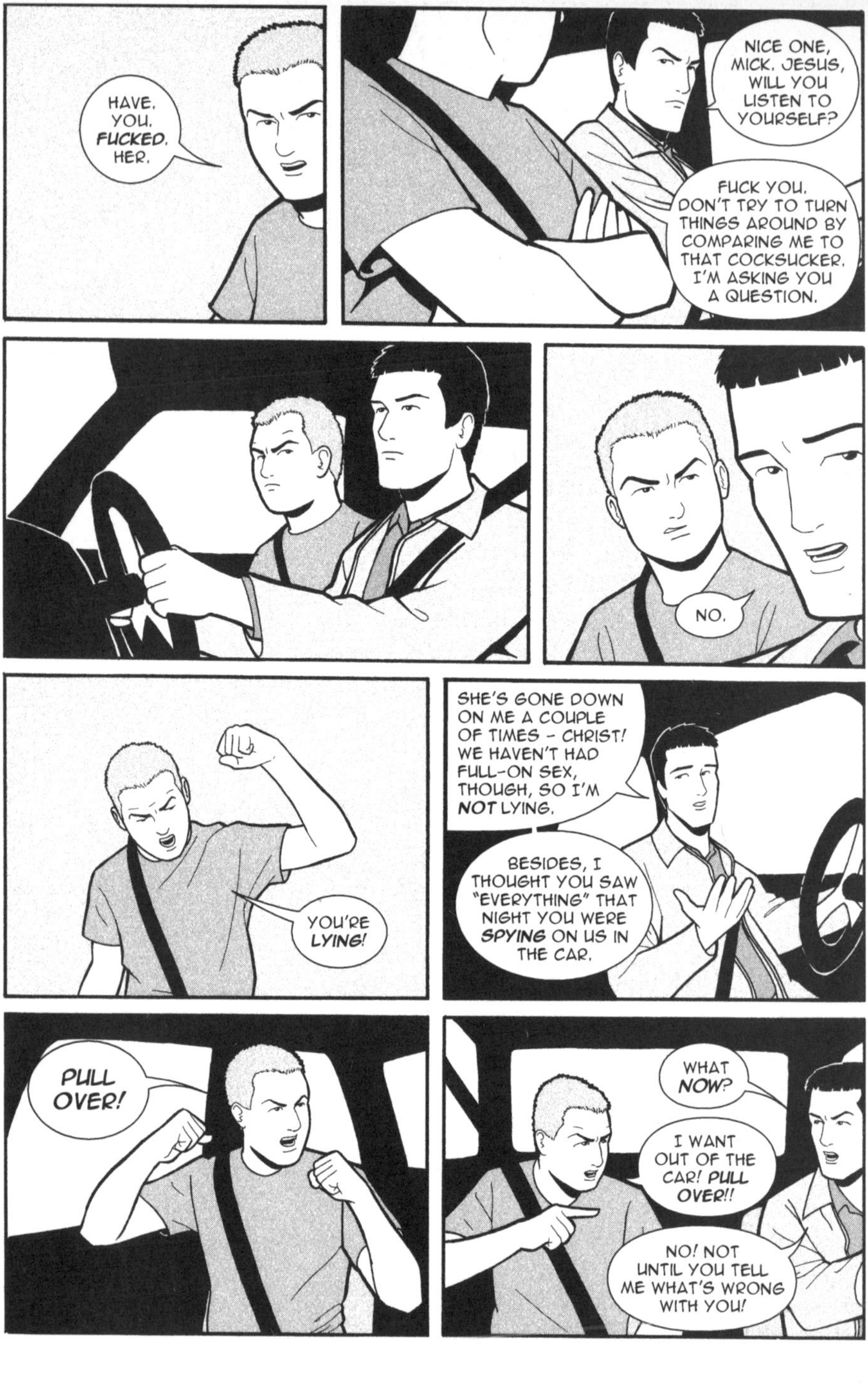
HAVE. YOU. **FUCKED.** HER.
NICE ONE, MICK. JESUS, WILL YOU LISTEN TO YOURSELF?
FUCK YOU. DON'T TRY TO TURN THINGS AROUND BY COMPARING ME TO THAT COCKSUCKER. I'M ASKING YOU A QUESTION.
NO.
YOU'RE ***LYING!***
SHE'S GONE DOWN ON ME A COUPLE OF TIMES - CHRIST! WE HAVEN'T HAD FULL-ON SEX, THOUGH, SO I'M ***NOT*** LYING.
BESIDES, I THOUGHT YOU SAW "EVERYTHING" THAT NIGHT YOU WERE ***SPYING*** ON US IN THE CAR.
PULL OVER!
WHAT ***NOW?***
I WANT OUT OF THE CAR! ***PULL OVER!!***
NO! NOT UNTIL YOU TELL ME WHAT'S WRONG WITH YOU!

PULL THE FUCK OVER OR I WILL HIT YOU SO HARD YOUR EYES SWITCH SOCKETS!
I SAW HER KISSING YOU, STEVE.
GETTING GRIFFIN TO DRIVE ME BY WAS HARD ENOUGH. HE WANTED TO LEAVE ALMOST AS SOON AS WE GOT THERE.
APPARENTLY WE LEFT BEFORE THE MAIN EVENT.

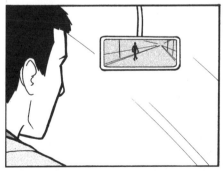

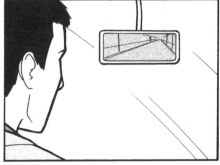

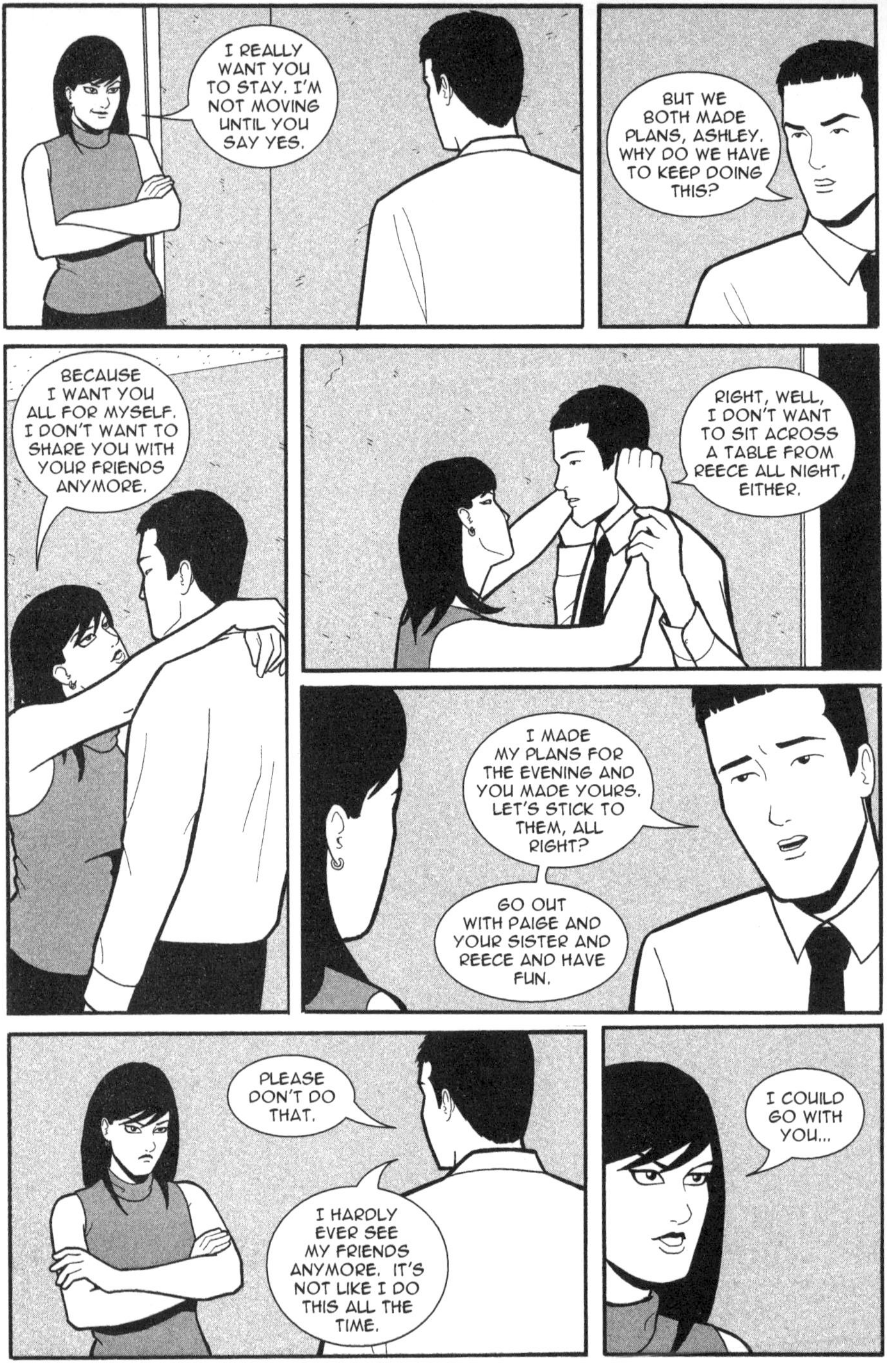
I REALLY WANT YOU TO STAY. I'M NOT MOVING UNTIL YOU SAY YES.
BUT WE BOTH MADE PLANS, ASHLEY. WHY DO WE HAVE TO KEEP DOING THIS?
BECAUSE I WANT YOU ALL FOR MYSELF. I DON'T WANT TO SHARE YOU WITH YOUR FRIENDS ANYMORE.
RIGHT, WELL, I DON'T WANT TO SIT ACROSS A TABLE FROM REECE ALL NIGHT, EITHER.
I MADE MY PLANS FOR THE EVENING AND YOU MADE YOURS. LET'S STICK TO THEM, ALL RIGHT?
GO OUT WITH PAIGE AND YOUR SISTER AND REECE AND HAVE FUN.
PLEASE DON'T DO THAT.
I HARDLY EVER SEE MY FRIENDS ANYMORE. IT'S NOT LIKE I DO THIS ALL THE TIME.
I COULD GO WITH YOU...

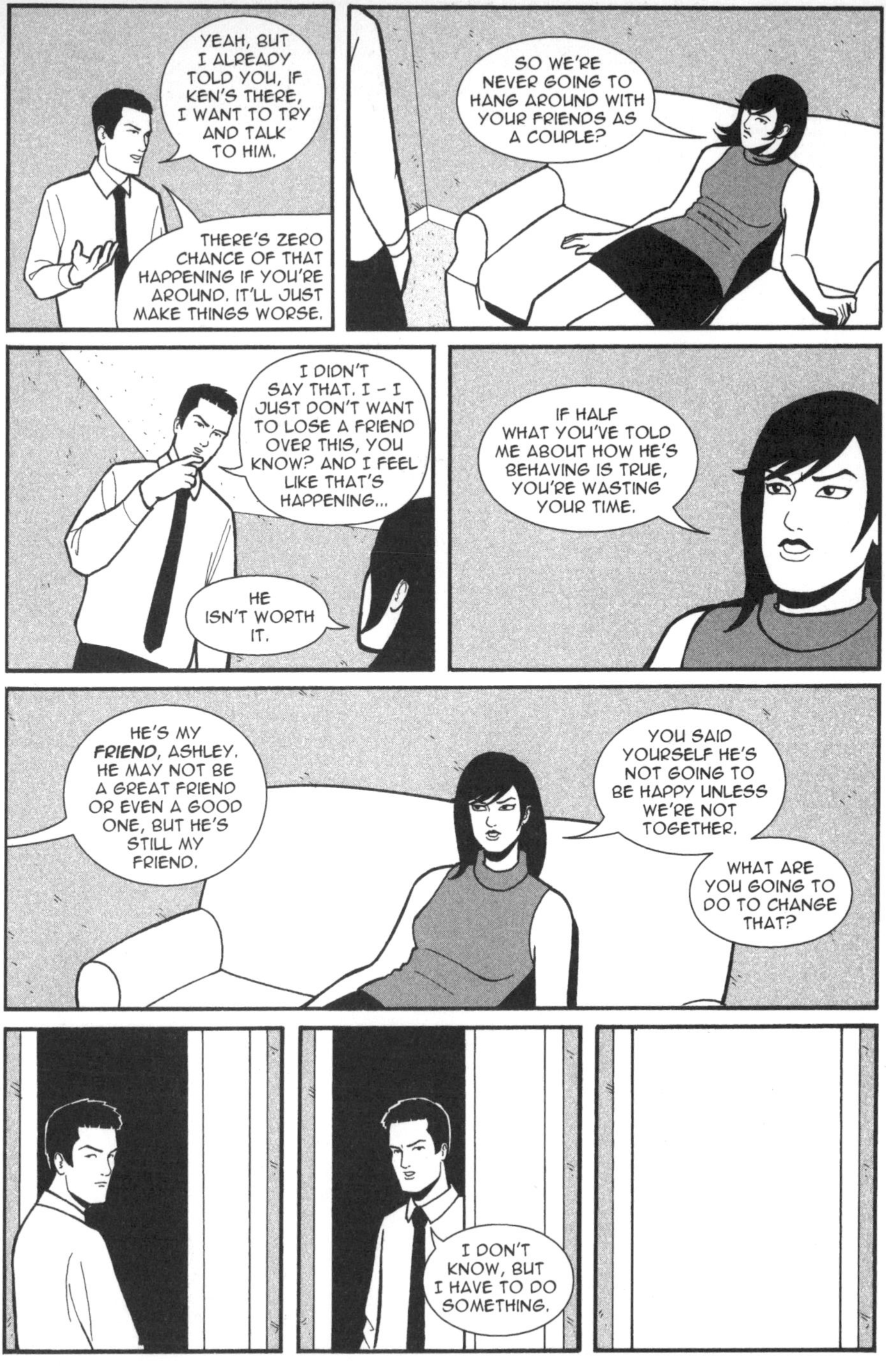
YEAH, BUT I ALREADY TOLD YOU, IF KEN'S THERE, I WANT TO TRY AND TALK TO HIM.
THERE'S ZERO CHANCE OF THAT HAPPENING IF YOU'RE AROUND. IT'LL JUST MAKE THINGS WORSE.
SO WE'RE NEVER GOING TO HANG AROUND WITH YOUR FRIENDS AS A COUPLE?
I DIDN'T SAY THAT. I - I JUST DON'T WANT TO LOSE A FRIEND OVER THIS, YOU KNOW? AND I FEEL LIKE THAT'S HAPPENING...
HE ISN'T WORTH IT.
IF HALF WHAT YOU'VE TOLD ME ABOUT HOW HE'S BEHAVING IS TRUE, YOU'RE WASTING YOUR TIME.
HE'S MY FRIEND, ASHLEY. HE MAY NOT BE A GREAT FRIEND OR EVEN A GOOD ONE, BUT HE'S STILL MY FRIEND.
YOU SAID YOURSELF HE'S NOT GOING TO BE HAPPY UNLESS WE'RE NOT TOGETHER.
WHAT ARE YOU GOING TO DO TO CHANGE THAT?
I DON'T KNOW, BUT I HAVE TO DO SOMETHING.

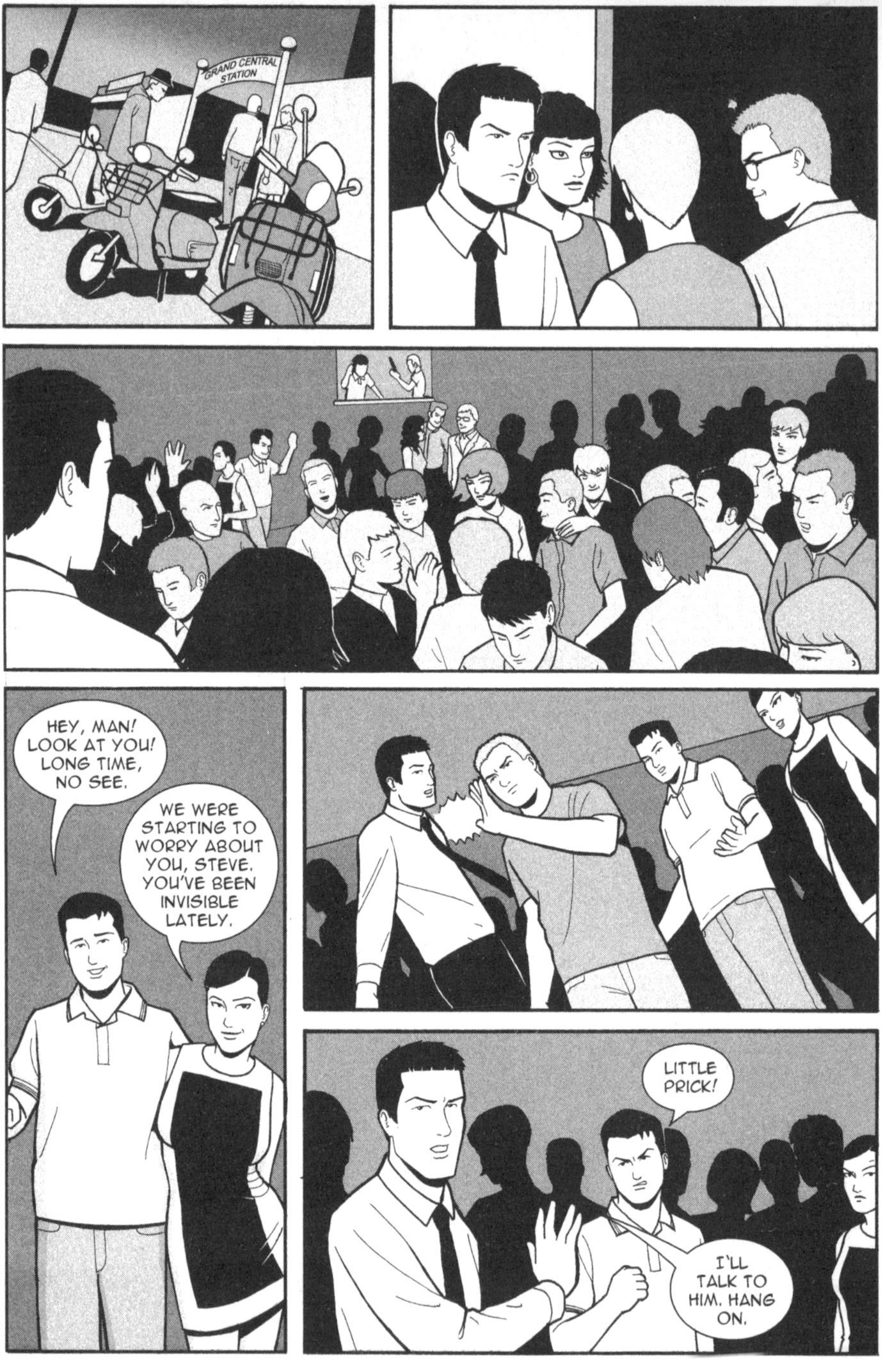
GRAND CENTRAL STATION
HEY, MAN! LOOK AT YOU! LONG TIME, NO SEE.
WE WERE STARTING TO WORRY ABOUT YOU, STEVE. YOU'VE BEEN INVISIBLE LATELY.
LITTLE PRICK!
I'LL TALK TO HIM. HANG ON.

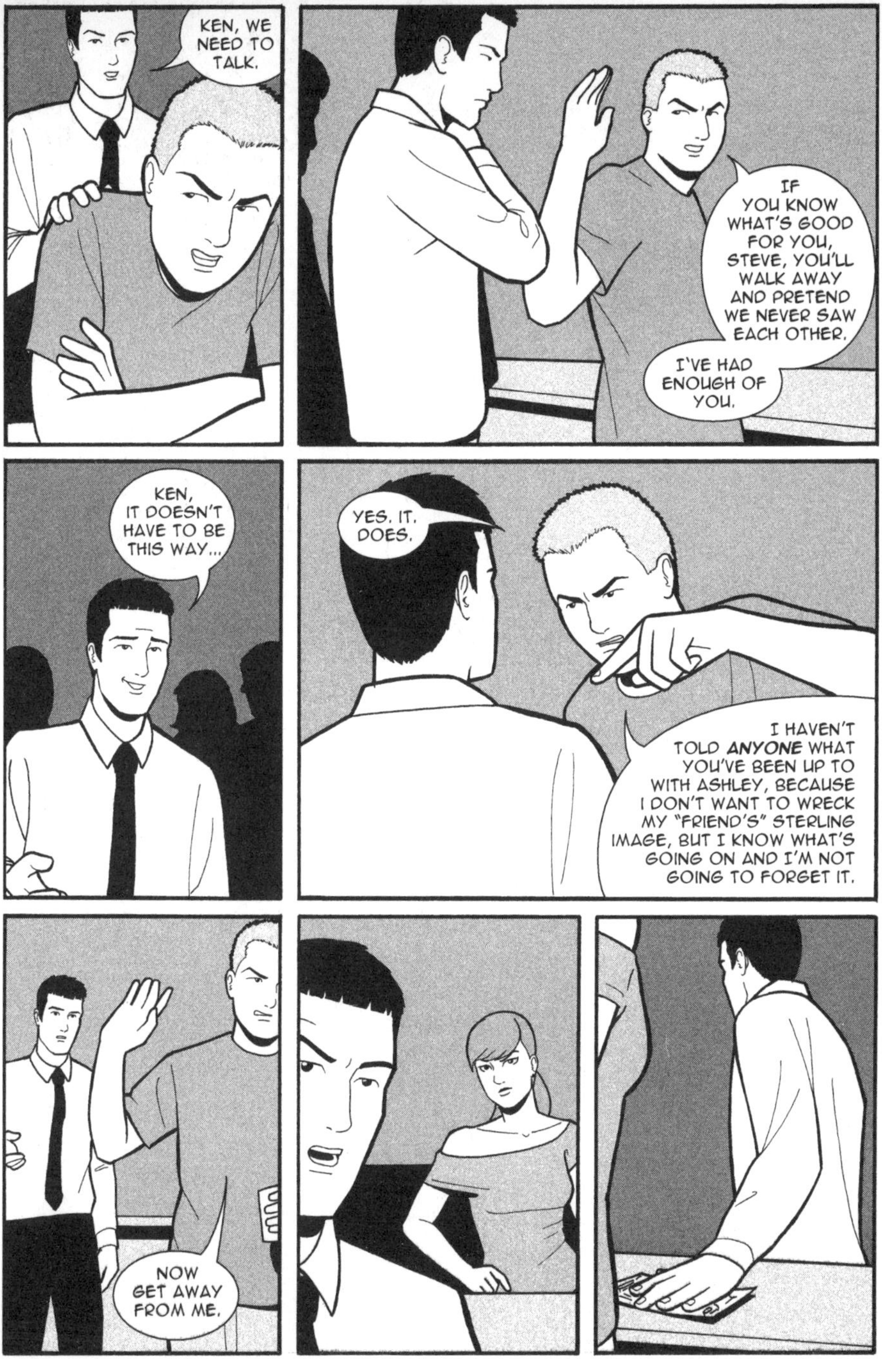
KEN, WE NEED TO TALK.
IF YOU KNOW WHAT'S GOOD FOR YOU, STEVE, YOU'LL WALK AWAY AND PRETEND WE NEVER SAW EACH OTHER.
I'VE HAD ENOUGH OF YOU.
KEN, IT DOESN'T HAVE TO BE THIS WAY...
YES. IT. DOES.
I HAVEN'T TOLD ***ANYONE*** WHAT YOU'VE BEEN UP TO WITH ASHLEY, BECAUSE I DON'T WANT TO WRECK MY "FRIEND'S" STERLING IMAGE, BUT I KNOW WHAT'S GOING ON AND I'M NOT GOING TO FORGET IT.
NOW GET AWAY FROM ME.

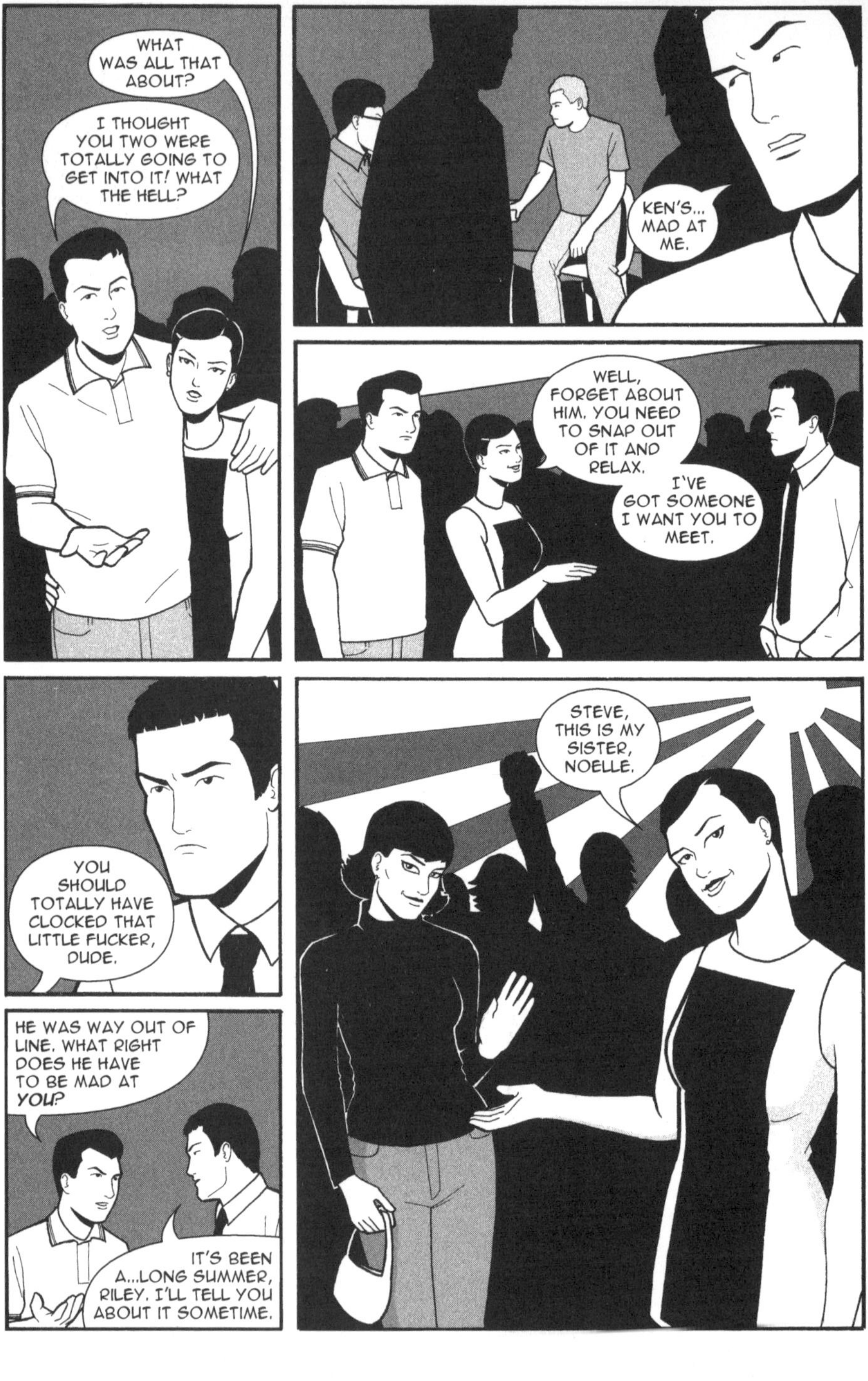
WHAT WAS ALL THAT ABOUT?
I THOUGHT YOU TWO WERE TOTALLY GOING TO GET INTO IT! WHAT THE HELL?
KEN'S... MAD AT ME.
WELL, FORGET ABOUT HIM. YOU NEED TO SNAP OUT OF IT AND RELAX.
I'VE GOT SOMEONE I WANT YOU TO MEET.
YOU SHOULD TOTALLY HAVE CLOCKED THAT LITTLE FUCKER, DUDE.
HE WAS WAY OUT OF LINE. WHAT RIGHT DOES HE HAVE TO BE MAD AT ***YOU***?
IT'S BEEN A...LONG SUMMER, RILEY. I'LL TELL YOU ABOUT IT SOMETIME.
STEVE, THIS IS MY SISTER, NOELLE.

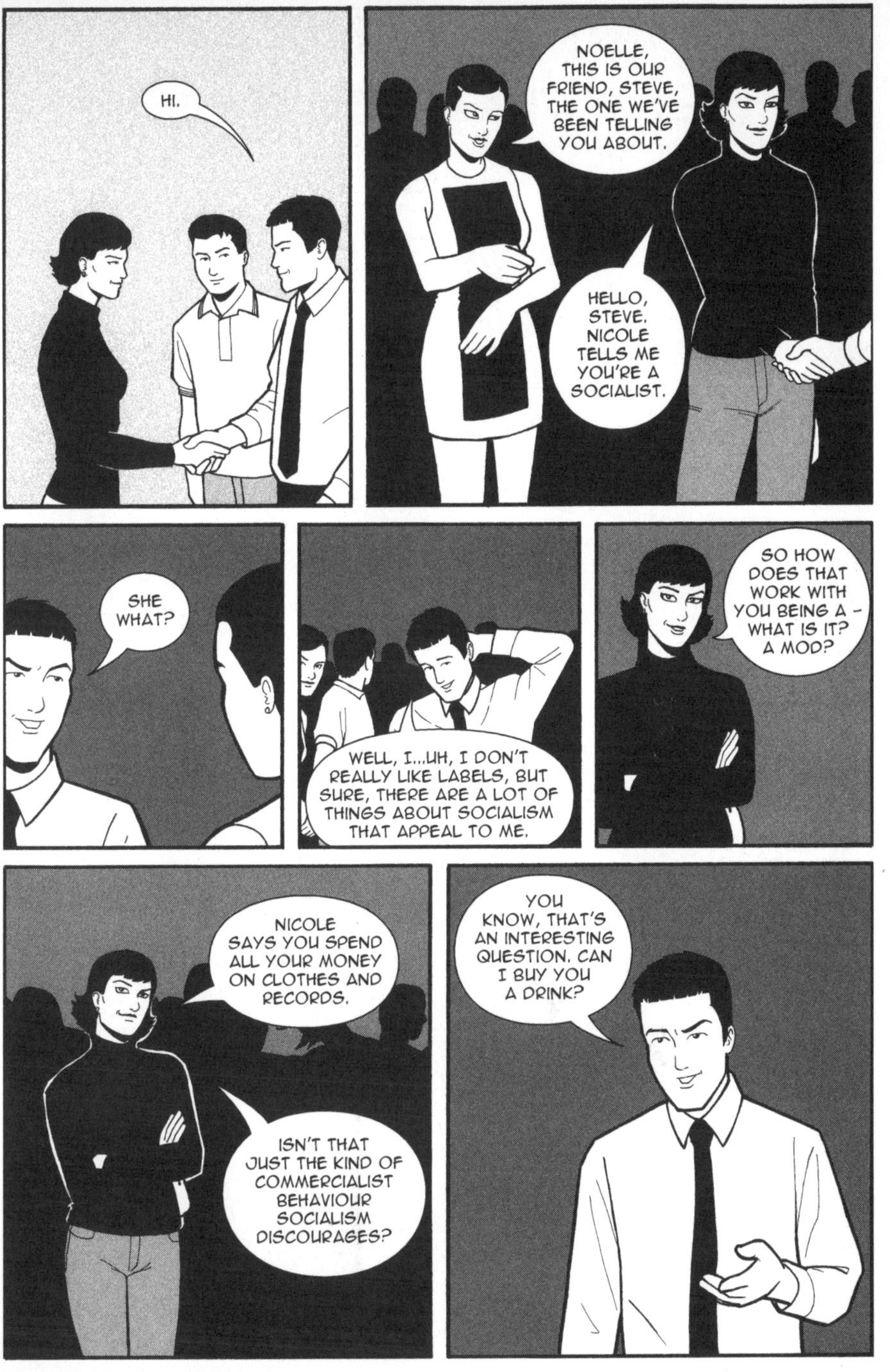
HI.
NOELLE, THIS IS OUR FRIEND, STEVE, THE ONE WE'VE BEEN TELLING YOU ABOUT.
HELLO, STEVE. NICOLE TELLS ME YOU'RE A SOCIALIST.
SHE WHAT?
WELL, I...UH, I DON'T REALLY LIKE LABELS, BUT SURE, THERE ARE A LOT OF THINGS ABOUT SOCIALISM THAT APPEAL TO ME.
SO HOW DOES THAT WORK WITH YOU BEING A - WHAT IS IT? A MOD?
NICOLE SAYS YOU SPEND ALL YOUR MONEY ON CLOTHES AND RECORDS.
ISN'T THAT JUST THE KIND OF COMMERCIALIST BEHAVIOUR SOCIALISM DISCOURAGES?
YOU KNOW, THAT'S AN INTERESTING QUESTION. CAN I BUY YOU A DRINK?

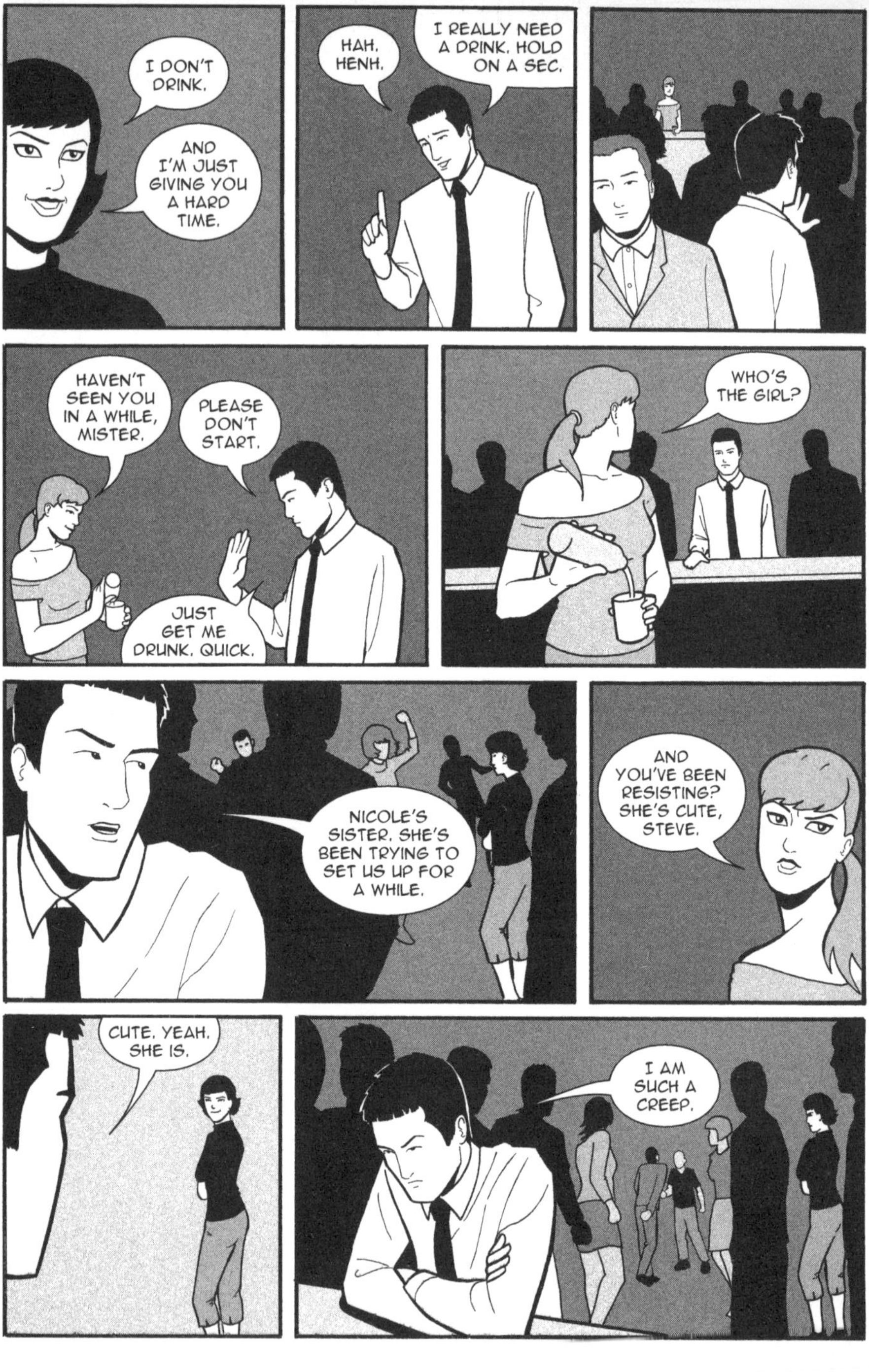
I DON'T DRINK.
AND I'M JUST GIVING YOU A HARD TIME.
HAH, HENH.
I REALLY NEED A DRINK. HOLD ON A SEC.
HAVEN'T SEEN YOU IN A WHILE, MISTER.
PLEASE DON'T START.
JUST GET ME DRUNK. QUICK.
WHO'S THE GIRL?
NICOLE'S SISTER. SHE'S BEEN TRYING TO SET US UP FOR A WHILE.
AND YOU'VE BEEN RESISTING? SHE'S CUTE, STEVE.
CUTE. YEAH. SHE IS.
I AM SUCH A CREEP.

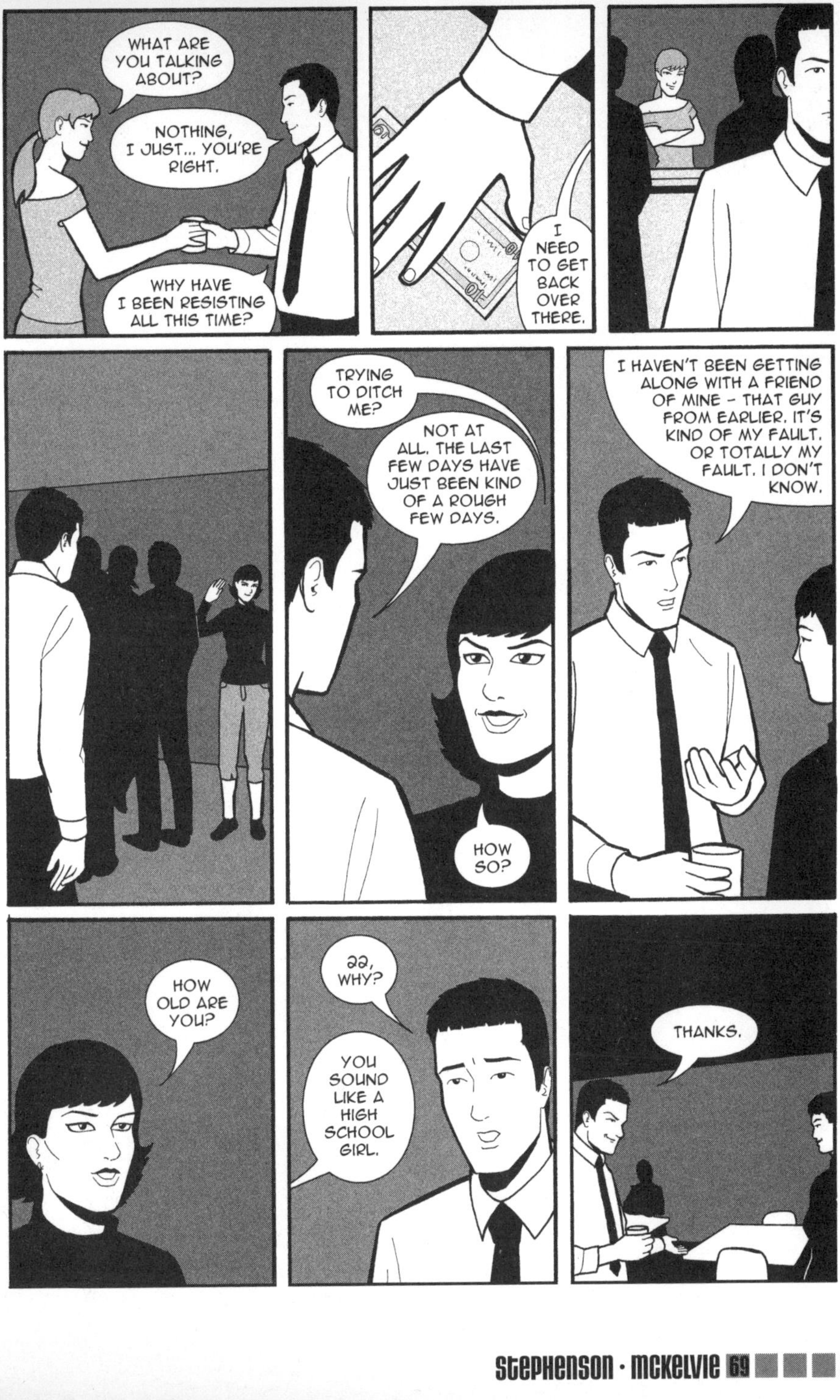
WHAT ARE YOU TALKING ABOUT?
NOTHING, I JUST... YOU'RE RIGHT.
WHY HAVE I BEEN RESISTING ALL THIS TIME?
I NEED TO GET BACK OVER THERE.
TRYING TO DITCH ME?
NOT AT ALL. THE LAST FEW DAYS HAVE JUST BEEN KIND OF A ROUGH FEW DAYS.
HOW SO?
I HAVEN'T BEEN GETTING ALONG WITH A FRIEND OF MINE - THAT GUY FROM EARLIER. IT'S KIND OF MY FAULT. OR TOTALLY MY FAULT. I DON'T KNOW.
HOW OLD ARE YOU?
22, WHY?
YOU SOUND LIKE A HIGH SCHOOL GIRL.
THANKS.

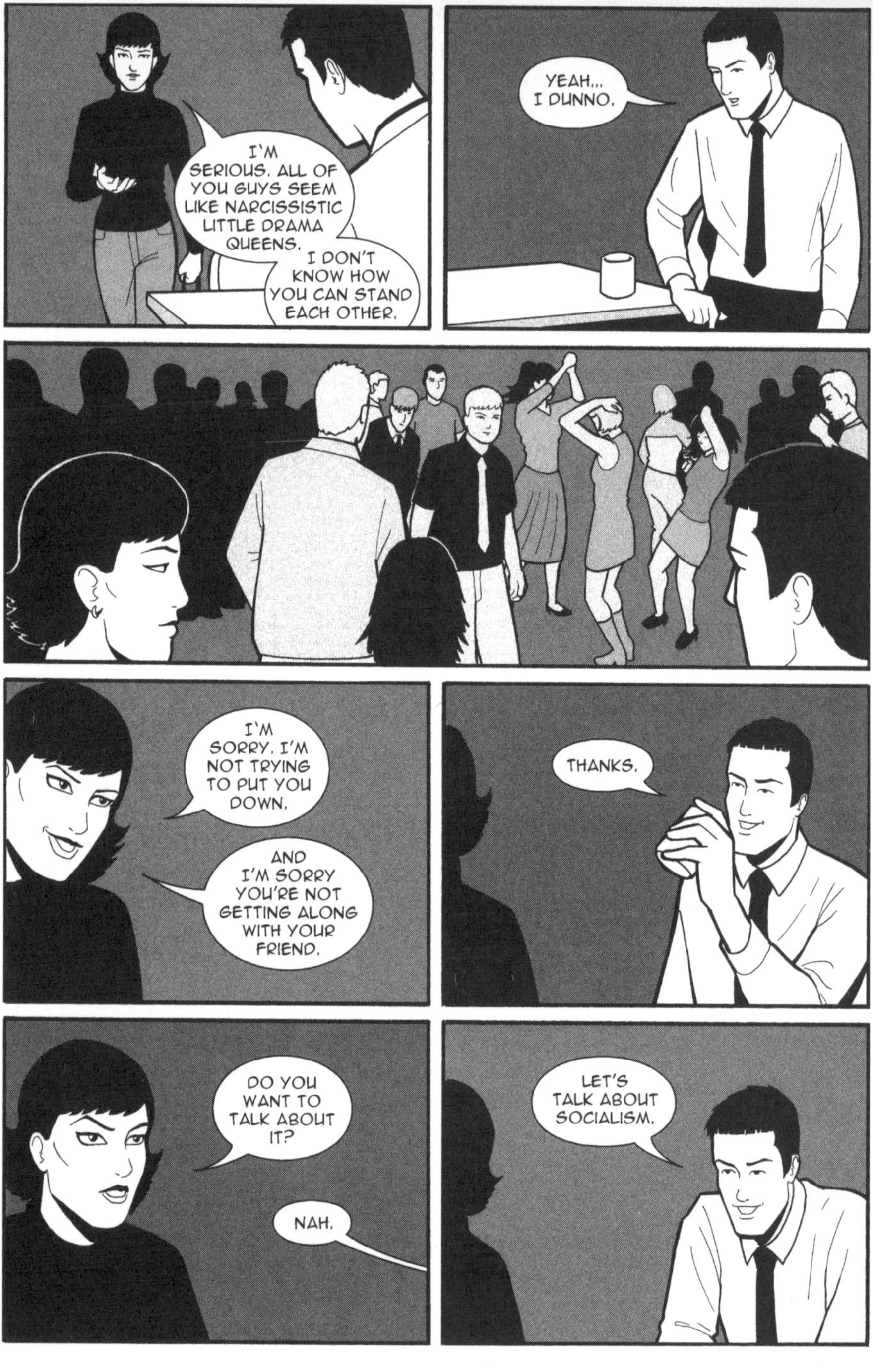
I'M SERIOUS. ALL OF YOU GUYS SEEM LIKE NARCISSISTIC LITTLE DRAMA QUEENS.
I DON'T KNOW HOW YOU CAN STAND EACH OTHER.
YEAH... I DUNNO.
I'M SORRY. I'M NOT TRYING TO PUT YOU DOWN.
AND I'M SORRY YOU'RE NOT GETTING ALONG WITH YOUR FRIEND.
THANKS.
DO YOU WANT TO TALK ABOUT IT?
NAH.
LET'S TALK ABOUT SOCIALISM.

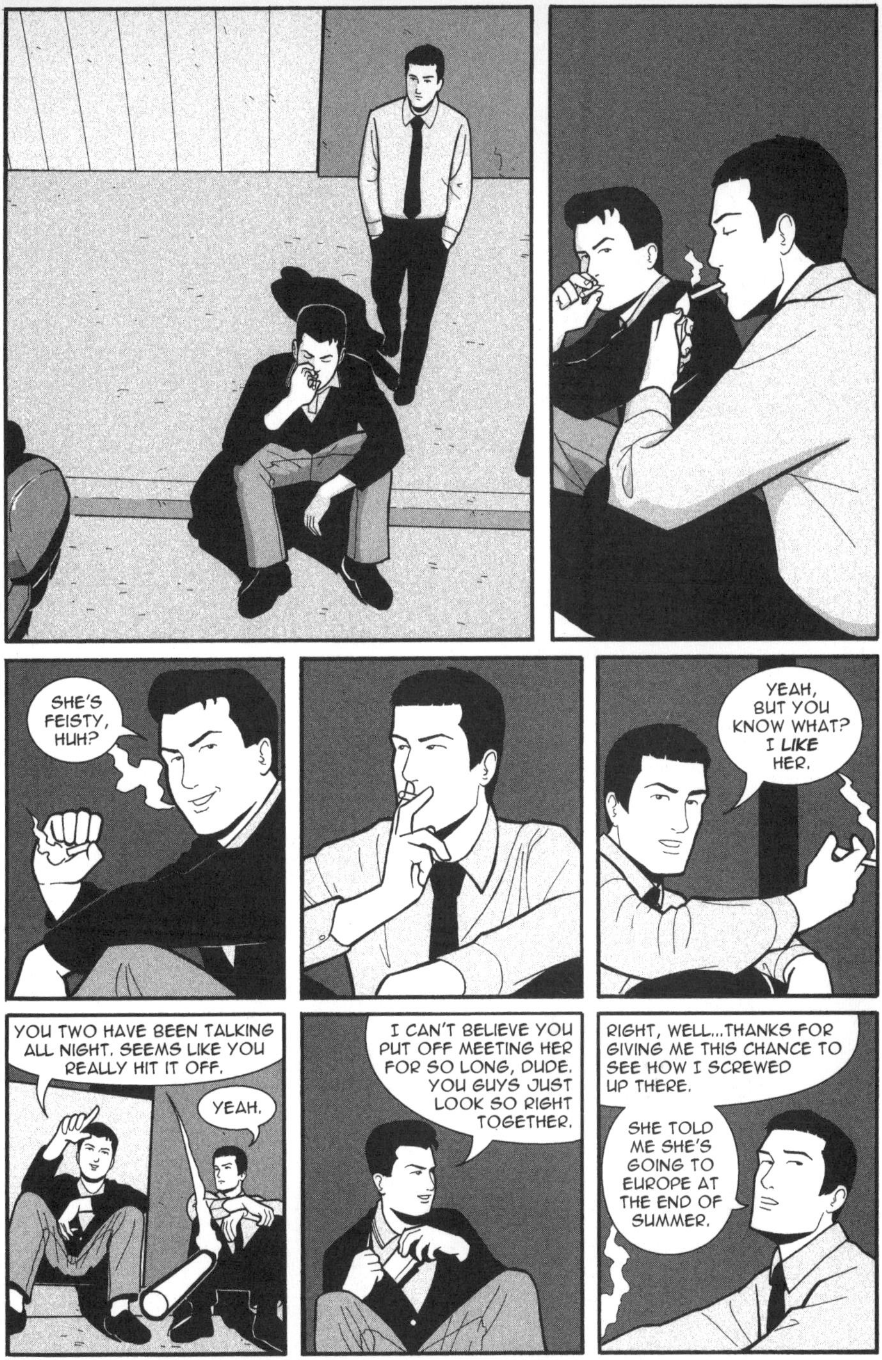
SHE'S FEISTY, HUH?
YEAH, BUT YOU KNOW WHAT? I **LIKE** HER.
YOU TWO HAVE BEEN TALKING ALL NIGHT. SEEMS LIKE YOU REALLY HIT IT OFF.
YEAH.
I CAN'T BELIEVE YOU PUT OFF MEETING HER FOR SO LONG, DUDE. YOU GUYS JUST LOOK SO RIGHT TOGETHER.
RIGHT, WELL...THANKS FOR GIVING ME THIS CHANCE TO SEE HOW I SCREWED UP THERE.
SHE TOLD ME SHE'S GOING TO EUROPE AT THE END OF SUMMER.

YEAH, BUT SHE'LL BE BACK EVENTUALLY, DUDE. IT'S NOT LIKE SHE'S GOING TO LIVE THERE THE REST OF HER LIFE.

YOU COULD SEND LETTERS...

I GUESS. I THINK WE CAN CALL THIS A MISSED OPPORTUNITY.

I'VE WASTED THIS WHOLE SUMMER.

WHAT DO YOU MEAN?

THAT THING IN THERE WITH KEN?

YEAH?

I'VE BEEN HANGING AROUND WITH THAT GIRL HE BROUGHT TO THE CLUB A WHILE BACK.

ANGIE?

ASHLEY.

RIGHT, ASHLEY.

AND HE JUST FOUND OUT?

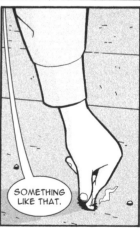

SOMETHING LIKE THAT.

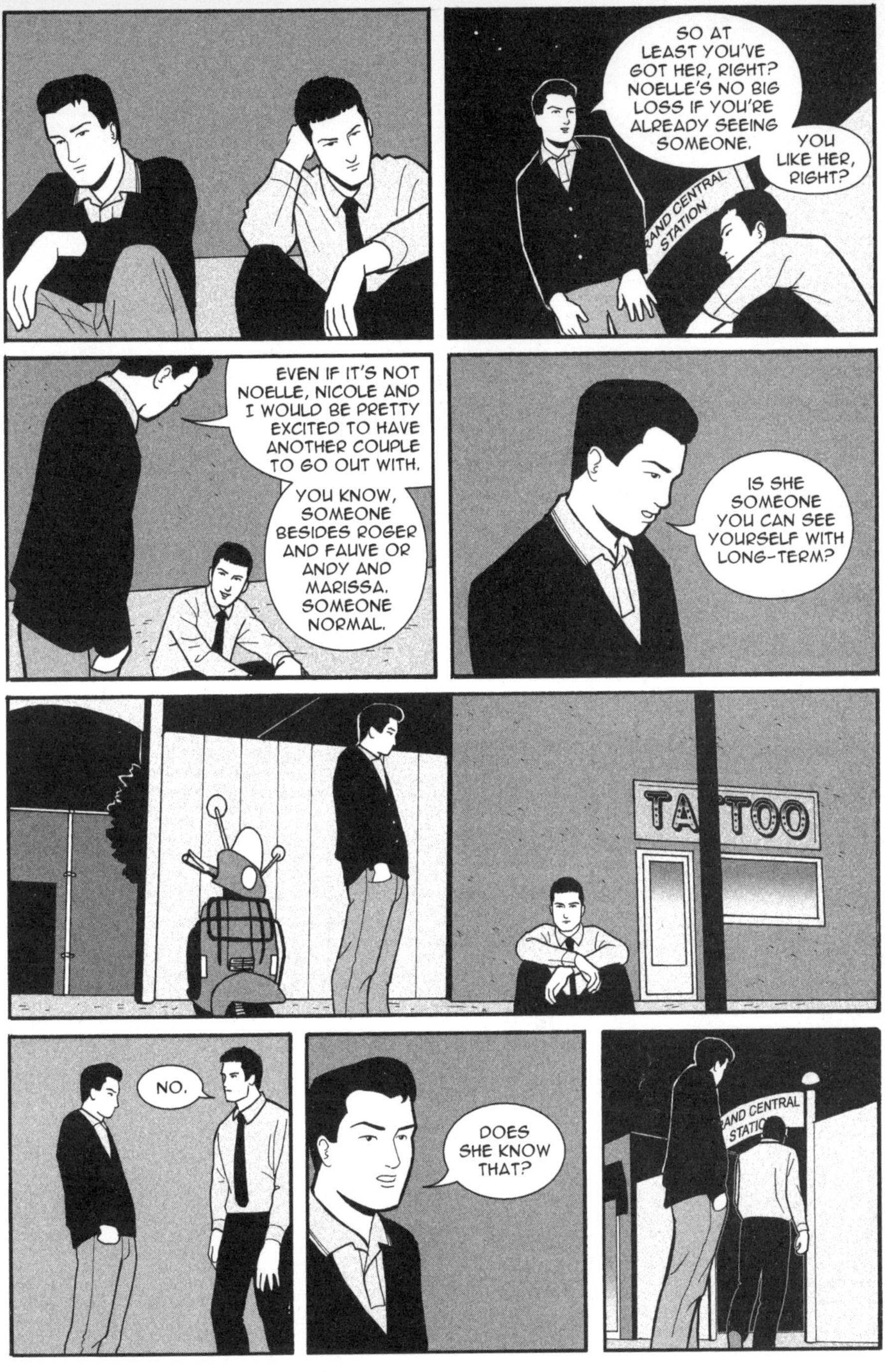
SO AT LEAST YOU'VE GOT HER, RIGHT? NOELLE'S NO BIG LOSS IF YOU'RE ALREADY SEEING SOMEONE.
YOU LIKE HER, RIGHT?
RAND CENTRAL STATION
EVEN IF IT'S NOT NOELLE, NICOLE AND I WOULD BE PRETTY EXCITED TO HAVE ANOTHER COUPLE TO GO OUT WITH.
YOU KNOW, SOMEONE BESIDES ROGER AND FAUVE OR ANDY AND MARISSA. SOMEONE NORMAL.
IS SHE SOMEONE YOU CAN SEE YOURSELF WITH LONG-TERM?
TATTOO
NO.
DOES SHE KNOW THAT?
RAND CENTRAL STATIO

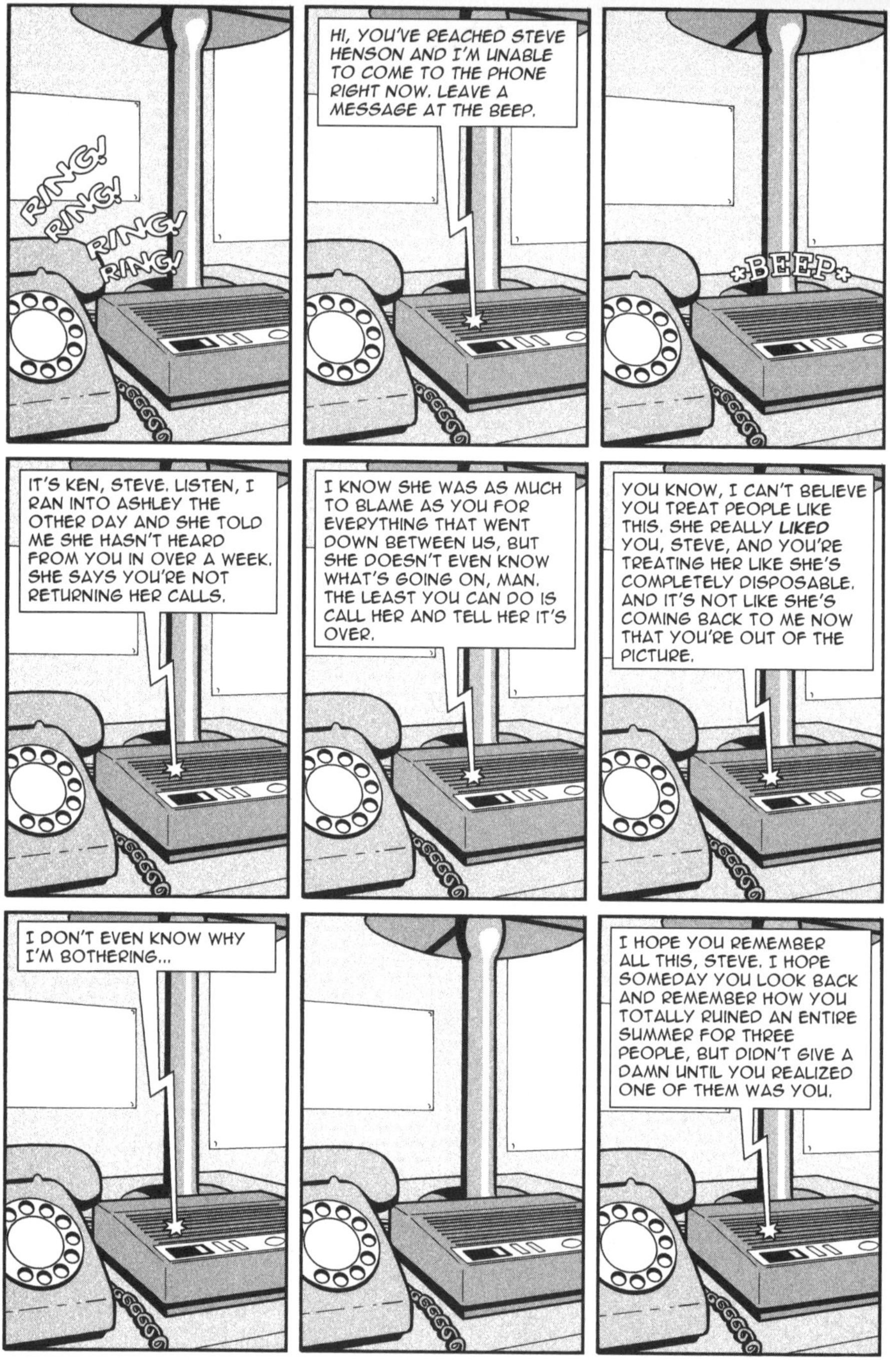
RING!
RING!
RING!
RING!
HI, YOU'VE REACHED STEVE HENSON AND I'M UNABLE TO COME TO THE PHONE RIGHT NOW. LEAVE A MESSAGE AT THE BEEP.
BEEP
IT'S KEN, STEVE. LISTEN, I RAN INTO ASHLEY THE OTHER DAY AND SHE TOLD ME SHE HASN'T HEARD FROM YOU IN OVER A WEEK. SHE SAYS YOU'RE NOT RETURNING HER CALLS.
I KNOW SHE WAS AS MUCH TO BLAME AS YOU FOR EVERYTHING THAT WENT DOWN BETWEEN US, BUT SHE DOESN'T EVEN KNOW WHAT'S GOING ON, MAN. THE LEAST YOU CAN DO IS CALL HER AND TELL HER IT'S OVER.
YOU KNOW, I CAN'T BELIEVE YOU TREAT PEOPLE LIKE THIS. SHE REALLY **LIKED** YOU, STEVE, AND YOU'RE TREATING HER LIKE SHE'S COMPLETELY DISPOSABLE. AND IT'S NOT LIKE SHE'S COMING BACK TO ME NOW THAT YOU'RE OUT OF THE PICTURE.
I DON'T EVEN KNOW WHY I'M BOTHERING...
I HOPE YOU REMEMBER ALL THIS, STEVE. I HOPE SOMEDAY YOU LOOK BACK AND REMEMBER HOW YOU TOTALLY RUINED AN ENTIRE SUMMER FOR THREE PEOPLE, BUT DIDN'T GIVE A DAMN UNTIL YOU REALIZED ONE OF THEM WAS YOU.

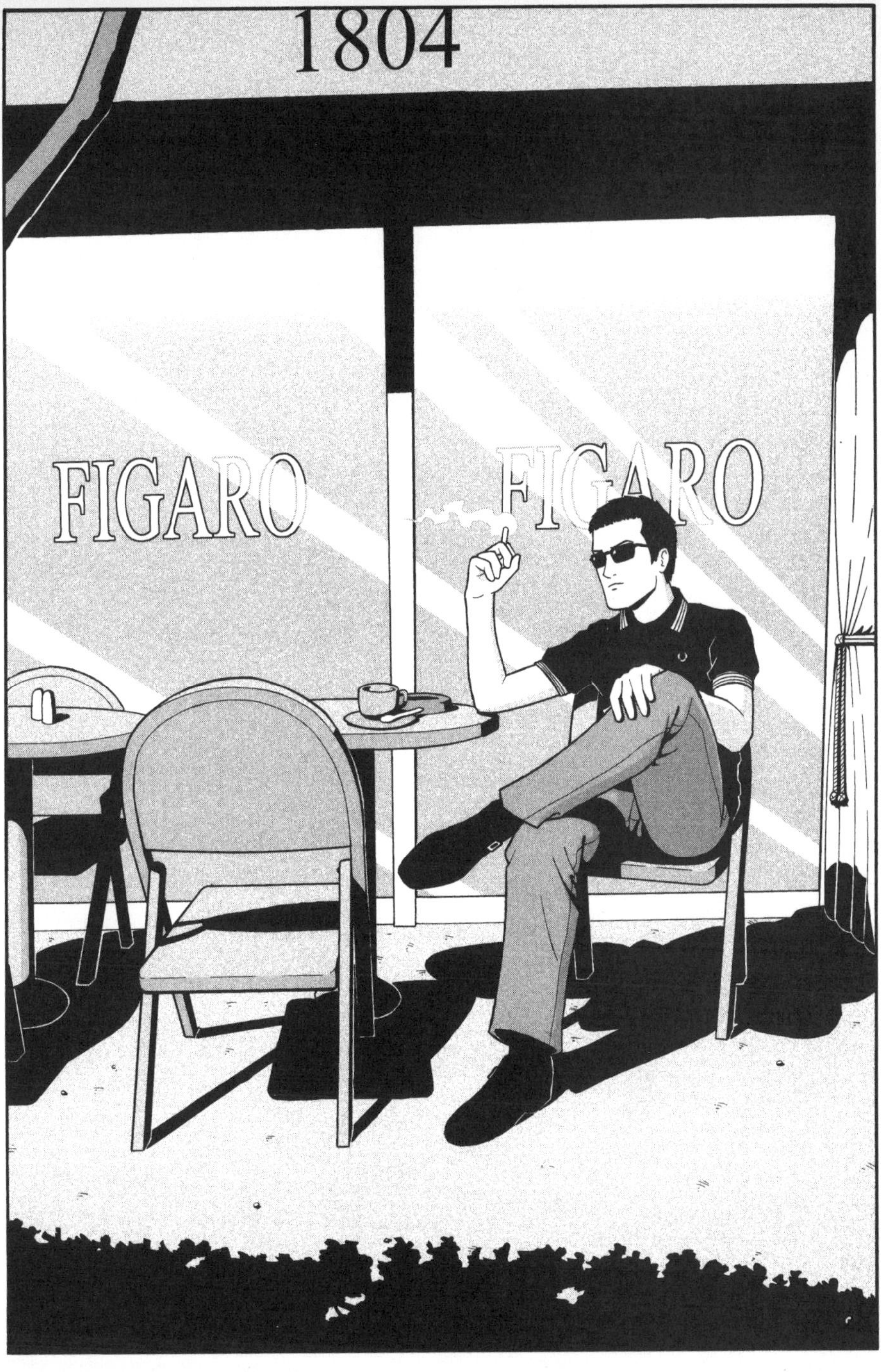
1804
FIGARO
FIGARO

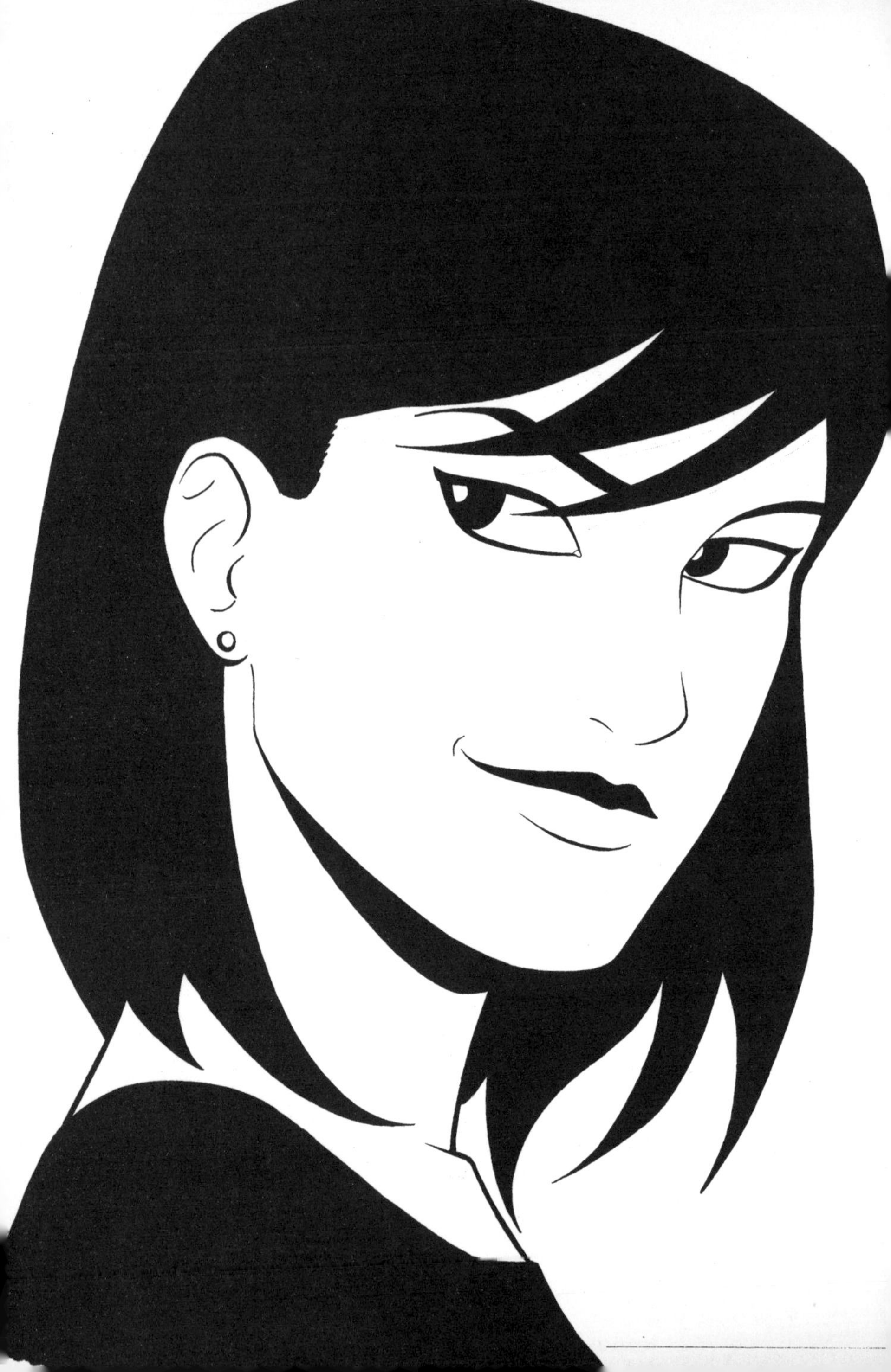

BIOS

Eric Stephenson

Eric Stephenson has been making comics, in one way or another, since 1991. His next project is NOWHERE MEN with artist Terry Stevens. He lives in San Francisco, but you can find him online at www.ericstephenson.com.

Jamie McKelvie

Jamie McKelvie lives in South London with his girlfriend, Fleur, and their ever-growing collection of action figures. LONG HOT SUMMER is his first full-length project following contributions to HOPELESS SAVAGES, BAD GIRLS, FOUR-LETTER WORLDS, NEGATIVE BURN and *UK OFFICIAL PLAY STATION MAGAZINE*. He has also done illustration work for *SPIN* and *KITCHEN SINK* magazines. Next up is his self-penned modern fantasy graphic novel, SUBURBAN GLAMOUR, due out sometime in the not-too-distant future from Image Comics.

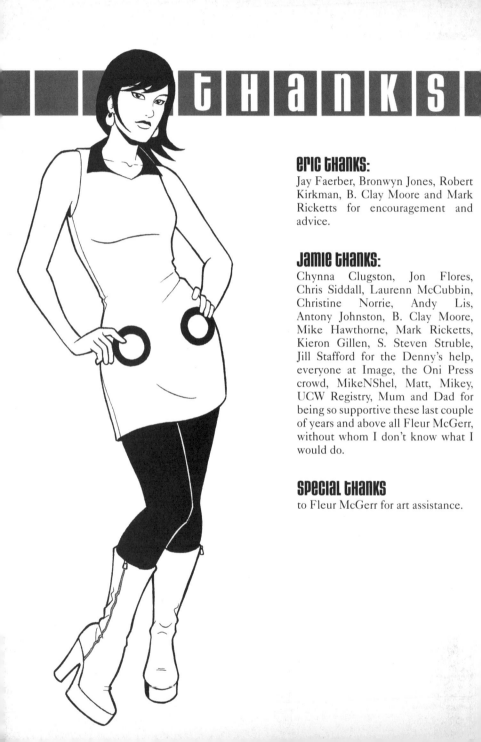

THANKS

eric thanks:

Jay Faerber, Bronwyn Jones, Robert Kirkman, B. Clay Moore and Mark Ricketts for encouragement and advice.

Jamie thanks:

Chynna Clugston, Jon Flores, Chris Siddall, Laurenn McCubbin, Christine Norrie, Andy Lis, Antony Johnston, B. Clay Moore, Mike Hawthorne, Mark Ricketts, Kieron Gillen, S. Steven Struble, Jill Stafford for the Denny's help, everyone at Image, the Oni Press crowd, MikeNShel, Matt, Mikey, UCW Registry, Mum and Dad for being so supportive these last couple of years and above all Fleur McGerr, without whom I don't know what I would do.

special thanks

to Fleur McGerr for art assistance.

more great BOOKS from image comics

40 OZ. COLLECTED TP
ISBN# 1582403298
$9.95

AGE OF BRONZE
VOL. 1:
A THOUSAND SHIPS TP
issues 1-9
ISBN# 1582402000
$19.95
VOL. 2:
SACRIFICE HC
issues 10-19
ISBN# 1582403600
$29.95

THE BLACK FOREST GN
ISBN# 1582403503
$9.95

CITY OF SILENCE TP
ISBN# 1582403678
$9.95

CLASSIC 40 OZ.:
TALES FROM THE
BROWN BAG TP
ISBN# 1582404380
$14.95

CREASED GN
ISBN# 1582404216
$9.95

DEEP SLEEPER TP
ISBN# 1582404933
$12.95

DIORAMAS,
A LOVE STORY GN
ISBN# 1582403597
$12.95

EARTHBOY JACOBUS GN
ISBN# 1582404925
$17.95

FLIGHT, VOL. 1 GN
ISBN# 1582403816
$19.95

FLIGHT, VOL. 2 GN
ISBN# 1582404771
$24.95

FOUR-LETTER WORLDS GN
ISBN# 1582404399
$12.95

GRRL SCOUTS
VOL. 1 TP
ISBN# 1582403163
$12.95
VOL. 2: WORK SUCKS TP
ISBN# 1582403430
$12.95

HAWAIIAN DICK, VOL. 1:
BYRD OF PARADISE TP
ISBN# 1582403171
$14.95

HEAVEN LLC. OGN
ISBN# 1582403511
$12.95

KANE
VOL. 1: GREETINGS FROM
NEW EDEN TP
issues 1-4
ISBN# 1582403406
$11.95
VOL. 2: RABBIT HUNT TP
issues 5-8
ISBN# 1582403554
$12.95
VOL. 3: HISTORIES TP
issues 9-12
ISBN# 1582403821
$12.95
VOL. 4: THIRTY NINTH TP
issues 13-18
ISBN# 1582404682
$16.95

LAZARUS CHURCHYARD
THE FINAL CUT GN
ISBN# 1582401802
$14.95

LIBERTY MEADOWS
VOL. 1:
EDEN LANDSCAPE ED TP
issues 1-9
ISBN# 1582402604
$19.95
VOL. 2:
CREATURE COMFORTS HC
issues 10-18
ISBN# 1582403333
$24.95

PUTTIN' THE BACKBONE
BACK TP (MR)
ISBN# 158240402X
$9.95

PvP
THE DORK AGES TP
original miniseries 1-6
ISBN# 1582403457
$11.95
VOL.1: PVP AT LARGE TP
issues 1-6
ISBN# 1582403740
$11.95
VOL. 2: PVP RELOADED TP
issues 7-12
ISBN# 158240433X
$11.95

REX MUNDI
VOL. 1: THE GUARDIAN OF
THE TEMPLE TP
issues 0-5
ISBN# 158240268X
$14.95
VOL. 2: THE RIVER UNDER-
GROUND TP
issues 6-11
ISBN# 1582404798
$14.95

SMALL GODS,
VOL. 1:
KILLING GRIN TP
issues 1-4
ISBN# 1582404577
$9.95

TOMMYSAURUS REX GN
ISBN# 1582403953
$11.95

ULTRA: SEVEN DAYS TP
ISBN# 1582404836
$17.95

THE WALKING DEAD
VOL. 1:
DAYS GONE BYE TP
issues 1-6
ISBN# 1582403589
$12.95
VOL. 2:
MILES BEHIND US TP
issues 7-12
ISBN# 1582404135
$12.95
VOL. 3:
SAFETY BEHIND
BARS TP
issues 13-18
ISBN# 1582404879
$12.95

THE WICKED WEST GN
ISBN# 1582404143
$9.95

®

For a comic shop near you carrying graphic novels from Image Comics, please call toll free: 1-888-COMIC-BOOK

WWW.IMAGECOMICS.COM

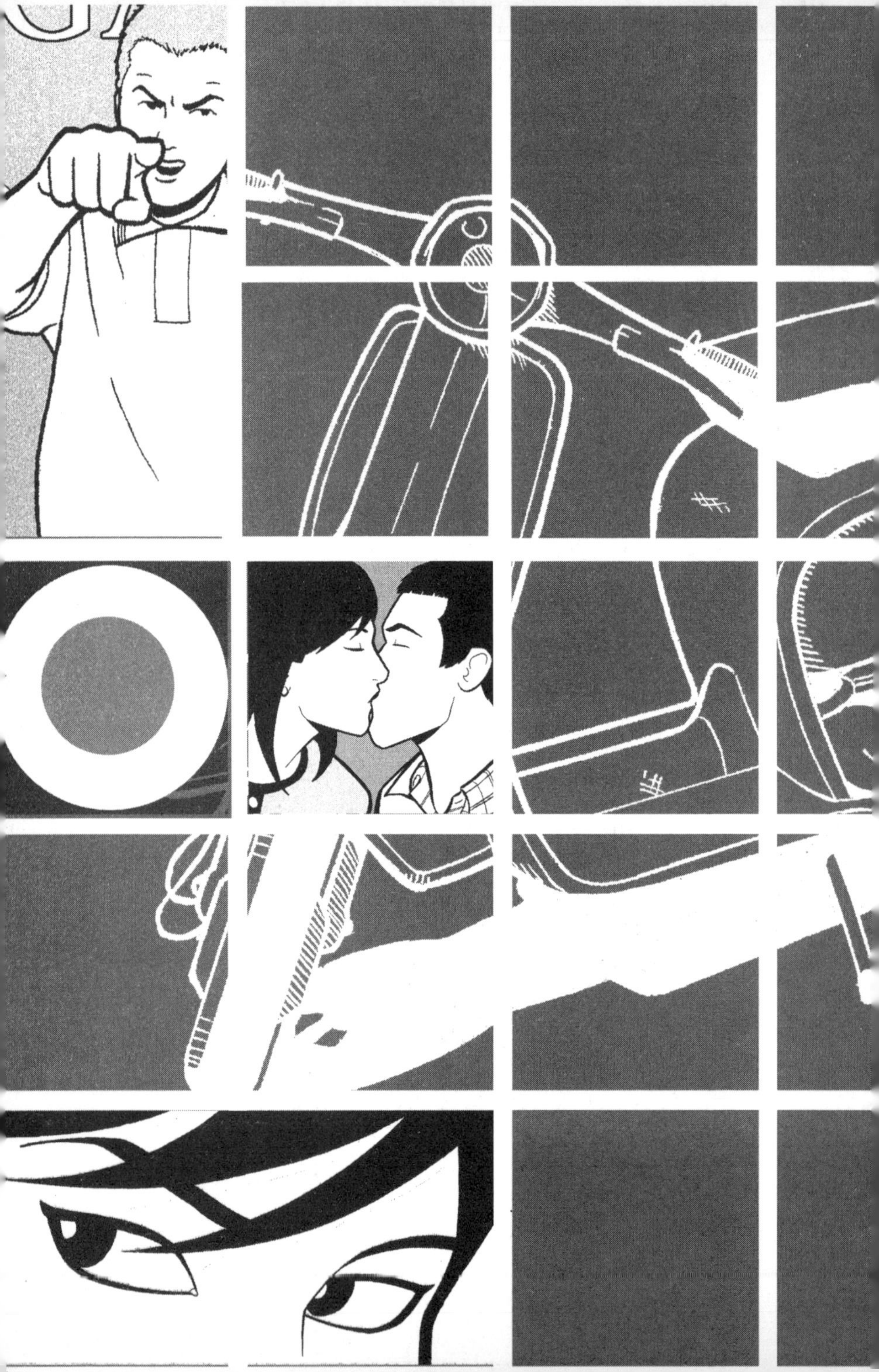